# The Non-Timing Trading System

# The Non-Timing Trading System

## A Rules-Based Conservative Trading System for Small Accounts

George O. Head

BUSINESS EXPERT PRESS

Leader in applied, concise business books

*The Non-Timing Trading System:*
*A Rules-Based Conservative Trading System for Small Accounts*

Copyright © Business Expert Press, LLC, 2021.

Cover design by Charlene Kronstedt

Interior design by Exeter Premedia Services Private Ltd., Chennai, India

First published in 2021 by
Business Expert Press, LLC
222 East 46th Street, New York, NY 10017
www.businessexpertpress.com

ISBN-13: 978-1-63742-004-1 (paperback)
ISBN-13: 978-1-63742-005-8 (e-book)

Business Expert Press Finance and Financial Management Collection

Collection ISSN: 2331-0049 (print)
Collection ISSN: 2331-0057 (electronic)

First edition: 2021

10 9 8 7 6 5 4 3 2 1

# Description

*The Non-Timing Trading System* is a conservative process for investing in the stock market. This book is perfect for the investors that are dissatisfied with low interest rates and want high returns on their investment without high risk. The book will teach you a low-risk strategy that will give you consistent average yearly returns between 20 percent and 30 percent and beat the S&P 500 year after year. The system is based on a mathematical model designed to protect your capital while giving you high returns.

You don't have to time the market and pick the right stock. The market will tell you what it is doing. There are always corrections in the market, even severe ones. The book describes in detail how it handles downturns and how it gets you out of the market before corrections become severe.

The author doesn't just show you a strategy and leave you hanging. There is a tutorial with five years of trading using the system which covers every possible scenario so that you are never left wondering what to do. Protection of your capital is its highest priority. The investor that is looking for high returns should not have to settle for high risk.

# Keywords

time the market; low risk; high return investing; stock market; options; option strategies; option trading; expected move; volatility

# Contents

# Introduction

Every investor wants high returns with low risk. In the past this was a paradox. If you wanted high returns you had to accept a much higher risk than you were comfortable with. This has changed with The Non-Timing Trading System. It is designed to give you average yearly returns of 20 percent to 30 percent consistently. And it will always beat the Standard & Poor's 500.

It is undeniable that the stock market has an upward bias. It will be higher tomorrow than it is today. The problem is that we don't know when that tomorrow is. It could be in a week, a month, or even longer. But it will be higher. The problem for the investor is how to take advantage of this upward bias without being subjected to the inevitable downturns and volatility of the market.

The Non-Timing Trading System is unlike any system or strategy that you have seen. It is based on a mathematical model that is designed to get you out of the market and keep you out during severe corrections or bear markets. At the same time it makes sure that you are in the market in order to take advantage of those uptrends that can make you a lot of money.

Trying to time the stock market is an impossible task. There are just too many factors. With this system you do not have to pick the right stock or time the market in order to be successful. Most investment strategies make you choose a direction. The stock market is going to do what it is going to do regardless of your opinion. Instead you will let the market tell you what it is doing, and you will always know what should be done. This is a conservative rules-based system. That means there are a set of rules that tell you what to do every step of the way as the stock market unfolds.

The Non-Timing Trading System uses options in order to control your risk. With options you have the ability to hedge your risk which will protect you from devastating losses; at the same time it will permit you to still have large gains. You will never be left with unlimited risk. Also options have predictive ability. They can't tell you in which direction a stock will go, but they can tell you with a high probability where you should close your position and take your profits or where you should accumulate additional positions.

Even if you know nothing about options, the chapter on options will teach you in easy-to-understand terms everything you need to know in order to be successful. There is even a section describing most of the major stock and option strategies. And it describes what their real risks are which is something that is often omitted.

A unique aspect of this book is its comprehensive tutorial. Many books on stock market strategies teach you a system and then assume that you understand all of its nuances with only a few examples. The tutorial chapter takes you through five years of actual simulated trades from November 1, 2013, through December 31, 2018. There is a complete explanation of each trade, why it was made, its effect, and the specific rule that applied. By the time you complete the tutorial you will have a thorough understanding of the system and any questions you might have had will be answered.

You can begin using The Non-Timing Trading System with as little as $500.00. And it is fully scalable to any size account without affecting its viability. Chapter 9 shows you step by step how to start. You can and should of course paper trade until you feel comfortable with any new system. But no matter how much you practice, if real money is not involved it is not the same emotionally and psychologically. But you don't have to risk a lot of money to get the true feeling of trading. By beginning with only $500.00 you are not risking so much that you cannot bring yourself to follow the rules. Once you have gained confidence in yourself and the system you can begin to increase the amount you are investing.

Remember, you can get high returns without high risk. Here's to successful investing.

# CHAPTER 1

# Let's Begin

I am the world's worst stock picker. If I buy a stock I guarantee you the next day it will go down. I am so bad at this I once shorted Amazon at $40 per share. Fortunately I got out of that one with my skin.

I've been investing in the stock and options market since the 1970s. You cannot imagine the amount of money that I have made and lost over that period of time. I believe I have tried and tested every system on the face of the earth. Over this period of time I've come to one undeniable conclusion:

*You cannot time the stock market!*

Warren Buffett has one simple system that has made him rich. He buys what he feels is a good company and then holds on.

But that can be just as risky for the average investor. Think Enron, Lehman Brothers, Eastern Airlines, and even the old General Motors. These were all "good" companies until they weren't. A strict buy-and-hold system can send you to the poor house just like every other system if you pick the wrong stocks.

Then what does work?

Let's start with some basic assumptions:

- The market generally goes up.
- There are bear markets and big corrections.
- You will never know when the market will begin to trend up or the bear will strike.
- You should be in the market at all times except in bear markets and big corrections.

The last one is the kicker. It looks like what is being advocated is buy-and-hold. But obviously you do not want to be long the market when you are in a bear market or a major correction. Later on we will discuss how you will know when to get out and stay out, and when you can get back in.

You might say that we are trying to find a method that can time the market. But that is not the case. We want to set up a set of rules that we will follow depending on what the market does. In that way the market is telling us what to do.

What you will see is that this is a simple low-risk rules-based system.

## Goals and Objectives

The goal of The Non-Timing Trading System is simple and modest. We not only want to beat the Standard & Poor's 500, but we want to increase our account by at least an average yearly minimum of 20 percent.

We want to accomplish this with a minimum amount of risk. Many books on trading try to determine your risk tolerance. I personally don't have much risk tolerance. I've been burned too many times. I want my average 20 percent per year without risk. But I am realistic enough to know that that is not going to happen. The only way to become truly risk free in the stock market is not to trade.

The Non-Timing Trading System will give you good average yearly returns of 20 percent to 30 percent. Of course it is not without risk, but the risk is low and always known.

There are systems out there that promise you 80 percent, 100 percent, or even 1,000 percent returns. There is even a system that says that you can get a 1,400 percent return in six days. Believe me when I tell you this cannot be done. At least those types of returns cannot be done safely. If you are not careful, systems like those can cause you to lose your entire investment capital.

Any system must be a rules-based system. Rules take emotion out of the situation. As long as you trust the rules and that they will protect you from devastating risk, then you are not left to your emotions and gut instinct. Emotions are what will get you into trouble.

In order to beat the S&P 500 and get an average yearly return of at least 20 percent you're going to need to have leverage. Generally leverage requires risk, and risk requires capital. We want a system that mitigates that risk, maintains the leverage, and can be used with as little as $500 of capital. It also needs to be upwardly scalable as needed.

## What the Non-Timing Trading System Is Not

First and foremost The Non-Timing Trading System is not a get rich quick system. You will not be constantly trading. It is designed to grind out a profit of at least an average yearly return of 20 percent to 30 percent. It is designed to put you into the market and keep you there in order to take advantage of the natural upward bias that the stock market has.

The problem with trying to time the market is that you never know when a trend will begin. By the time you recognize that you are in a major uptrend you have generally been left on the sidelines and find yourself trying to play catch-up.

But at the same time you do not want to be in the market during a major correction or a bear market. Just as you will never know when a major uptrend is beginning, you will also never know when a major downtrend is beginning. Therefore we have rules that will get you out of the market when things are not acting right and then get you back in when the market has stabilized. These rules are based upon the assumption that it is better to miss an opportunity than to lose your account.

## What Are the Risks?

In The Non-Timing Trading System the risk will always be defined. There will never be a time where you will have unlimited risk. That is not to say that you cannot lose money. You can. In fact depending on the strategy that you employ, part of that trade will generally lose some money.

As I talk about how risk is controlled I will be making a reference to option strategies that you may not understand at this point. Do not be concerned. All this will be thoroughly explained in the option tutorial. For those that have a basic understanding of options and basic option strategies, this is pretty basic and is not difficult to understand.

The main vehicle that we're going to use is the vertical call spread. This is where you will buy a lower strike price option and sell a higher strike price option. In this way we can control the amount of risk at any point in time.

In a market that goes up the lower strike price that we bought will gain in value at a faster rate, and the higher strike price that we sold will lose its value at a lower rate. The reason for this is that the lower strike price that we bought has a higher Delta than the higher strike price that we sold.

The vertical spread has one main disadvantage. Even though we are limiting our losses, we are also capping our gains. There is an absolute cap on the amount of money that we can make. But we're going to set the distance between the strike price that we buy and the strike price that we sell so that this cap is never reached before the upper limit is reached and the system tells us that we need to close out the position.

Another reason we will use a vertical spread is that we want to be able to control the cost of the unit. We want a single unit to be approximately 10 percent of our capital allocation. If the capital allocation is $5,000 then a single unit will cost about $500. If your capital allocation is $500, then your single unit would be somewhere around $50.

We also want the strike price that we buy to be around the At the Money strike. Since the main vehicle that we will be using is the SPY (SPY is the stock symbol for an ETF or Exchange Traded Fund which mirrors the S&P 500.), the At the Money strike on the SPY generally is substantially more than $500. That makes it very difficult to control the number of units that we need to buy depending on the situation. In high volatility this can get totally out of control. So when we sell the higher strike price option we are receiving a credit which will offset the cost of the At the Money option and thus lower our overall cost and risk.

## What Will You Need?

There are several things that you're going to need:

In all of the examples in the book we use a basic capital allocation of $5,000. This is based on the width of our spread being 10 points. With a 10-point vertical spread on the SPY, we will be putting at risk about $500 to $600 per unit. A unit will be explained later. If your capital is less there is a section which explains the spread adjustment that you will use. Obviously with less capital to invest you won't make as much money of course, but it will still meet the goals of the system, to make at least an average yearly return of 20 percent to 30 percent and to beat the Standard & Poor's 500.

In our example portfolio, in order to be the most conservative, the beginning $5,000 allocation will decrease if losses are incurred. If profits are made we do not increase the $5,000 available. This is not to say that you shouldn't invest more as more capital is available to you. It is just that the examples here that we use are based on the assumption that at any point in time you only have a maximum of $5,000 available to you.

You will also need a brokerage account. This should be an online brokerage account. We use in our examples the Think or Swim software from TD Ameritrade and Charles Schwab. Other online brokerages will have similar capabilities. And regardless of the brokerage that you use, you should have access to all of the essential tools that are described here.

You will also need to have the ability to trade options. Once you open your brokerage account you will need to make sure that it is a margin account. A margin account typically gives you the ability to borrow money from your broker in order to buy stock. We are never going to be borrowing money, and you will never owe money to your broker using The Non-Timing Trading System. And as such you will never be paying interest. But regulations require that options may only be traded in a margin account.

Once the margin account is opened you will have to make an application to trade options. Most brokerages have three levels of option trading. Level I permits you only to do covered calls. Level II permits you to do a variety of option strategies including buying and selling vertical spreads. This is because vertical spreads whether you are the buyer or the seller have a limited risk. Level III permits you to sell naked puts and calls. Selling a naked put or call exposes you to an unlimited risk. You will need of course to apply for Level II.

You will also need to have a basic understanding of how options are traded. You need to have a thorough understanding of how to trade puts and calls, what they are, risk graphs, intrinsic and extrinsic values, the Greeks especially Delta and Theta, spreads, assignments and expirations, and other interesting concepts such as expected move. The next chapter will teach you everything you need to know about all of this.

Even if you have a good understanding of options and how they are traded, you might still want to take a look at Chapter 2. You may skim over the parts that you thoroughly understand. Do pay attention to the discussion of volatility and expected moves. This plays an integral part in the system.

# CHAPTER 2

# Basic Option Tutorial

## The Metaphor of the House

In order to understand what an option is, let's relate it to something in the real world. Most are familiar with how real estate works. In real estate there are basically two ways to make money. You can buy the property, live in it, wait a long time, then sell the property, hopefully at a profit. The second way to make money in real estate is to buy the property and rent it out. This brings in an income from the rents regardless of the value of the property. If later you sell the property for a profit then so much the better. But the real income was from the rent, not necessarily from the future appreciation of the property.

The problem with renting the property is that during that time you don't get to enjoy the use of the property and generally cannot do with it as you please. How could you create an income flow from the property and at the same time maintain all the use, rights, and benefits of the property? There actually is a way.

Let's assume you buy a house for $120,000. Shortly after purchasing the house, someone comes to you and says that they would like to buy your house, but not now. What they offer is to buy an option on the house from you. Here's how it would work.

They will give you $10,000 for the right to buy your house anytime within one year for $125,000. Here's what the contract means. You get $10,000 now. That $10,000 is yours to keep no matter what happens. If the value of the house goes up during the year then the option purchaser has the right, not the obligation, to purchase your house at any time during the year for $125,000.

Let's say that the value of the house goes to $180,000. Then sometime during the year the option purchaser will force you to sell the house for $125,000. In that event you not only get the $5,000 profit on the sale of the house, but you also get to keep the $10,000 option money that was given to you upfront. Remember you only paid $120,000 for the house. Therefore you made a $15,000 profit on the property.

On the other hand, if the property does not appreciate in value, then at the end of the year, assuming that the value of the house has not changed and is still worth $120,000, the option purchaser would not exercise his right to buy it for $125,000. Therefore you will keep the house, and you get to keep the $10,000 option money. In any event you have made at least $10,000 on the house in a year.

In essence you have rented the house out for the year without the hassles of dealing with tenants, and you got to enjoy the benefits of the house at the same time. Remember though that during the period of the option on the house, you do not have total control of the house. You do not have a right to sell the house during that period. The option owner in essence controls that aspect of your house. The only way that you could sell the house during the period of the option contract would be if you bought the option back from the purchaser. Depending on the value of the house at the time, you may have to pay more or could pay less than the original $10,000 to get out of the contract.

You might say that this is not a bad deal for the property owner. But who in his right mind would buy an option such as this on a piece of property? Let's look at it from the point of view of the purchaser of the option. We already understand how you will make out from such a deal.

If the purchaser has some kind of information or simply a good hunch and thinks that the value of the house within one year will go to $180,000, then in essence for $10,000 he can control that property during the year. If the house does go to $180,000 he simply exercises his option and buys the house for $125,000 and then immediately resells the house for $180,000. Now he has a nice profit of $45,000 ($180,000–$125,000–$10,000 = $45,000).

Notice that in order for the purchaser of the option to break even on the deal, the value of the house must appreciate at least to $135,000. In other words it has to increase first to the $125,000 purchase price, then another $10,000 to pay for the cost of the option. Remember that you get to keep the $10,000 option money regardless of what happens.

What then is your risk as the option seller? If the property appreciates you have no risk of loss. The only thing that you are giving up is the possibility of making a larger profit than the $15,000 which you will receive if the property appreciates higher than $135,000. No matter how high the value of the property goes, you are limited to a profit of $10,000 on the option plus $5,000 on the appreciated sale of the house. Therefore your risk on the upside is simply a loss of opportunity for more profit. What you are getting then is a bird in the hand. You are making your money upfront on the rental of the house through options rather than tenants. You are giving up the speculation on the future appreciation of the house.

What happens then if the house does not appreciate in value. Assume that the value stays between $120,000 and $125,000. What happens is that the option expires worthless and you get to keep the $10,000, and you can do it again for another $10,000 for the next year if you can find someone to buy the option.

The third possibility is that the value of the house declines. Let's assume that the value of the house goes down to $110,000. This is where your real risk exists. Obviously the option will not be exercised, and you will get to keep the $10,000. But now if you try to sell another option where the purchaser buys your house for $125,000, you are not going to get as much for the option since the value of the house is $110,000 rather than when the house had a value of $120,000.

In addition at the end of the option contract, if you were to have to sell the house at this time let's say for personal reasons, then you would take a $10,000 loss on the house. But at least that loss is made up by the option money that you received. Another way of looking at it is that you incur that downside risk any time you buy property. The difference is that you at least have the $10,000 in option money to soften that downside risk. It is $10,000 more than you would have had if you had simply bought the property and held it without selling the option in the hopes that the property would appreciate.

This is all well and good as a metaphor with real estate to help understand how options work. But how on earth do you find people who are willing to buy options on property? In real estate it's not easy at all. In fact it's next to impossible. You would have to be sitting on just the right property and have a lot of connections to cut a deal as I have described.

Now let's turn to stocks. Here it's not difficult to find buyers who are willing to pay money in order to control your stock for a given period of time. In fact there is an option exchange where options on stocks are bought and sold through brokerages. It's as easy as selling and buying stock. In fact a market order for an option on the buy or sell side can be executed in a matter of seconds. So you don't have to go hunting for buyers.

## The Call Option

What was described in "The Metaphor of the House" is a call option. A call option gives the buyer the right, not the obligation, to purchase a stock at a specific price within a specific time period.

Here's how it works. Let's start with the assumption that you have purchased XYZ stock at $30 per share. You want to sell a one-month option on that stock for $2.00 per share. Assuming that you purchased 1,000 shares of stock then you have invested $30,000 for XYZ stock at $30 per share.

You get a quote on the price of a one-month option at 30 (the price for which the option purchaser has the right to purchase your stock), and you find the 30 option is worth $2.00. Each option contract is for 100 shares of stock. Since you own 1,000 shares you can sell 10 contracts (10 × 100). You tell your broker to sell 10 one-month 30 option contracts at $2.00. So $2,000 (2 × 10 × 100) is now deposited into your account. That $2,000 is yours to keep no matter what happens just like the option money on the real estate.

One month passes by. Remember that the term of the option was one month. At the end of one month assume that the stock price is more than $30 per share. Your stock will be *called* away from you, meaning that you will have to sell the stock at $30 per share. This is the same price you paid for it. In that event you break even on the stock and make $2,000 for one month on your $30,000 investment.

On the other hand let's assume that the stock price stays the same. At the end of the month the stock price is $30 per share. In that case your stock will not be called away. You will get to keep your stock and you get to keep the $2,000. Now you can sell options for another month against the stock.

The third possibility is that at the end of the month the stock has declined to $28 per share. Your stock will not be called away and you get to keep the $2,000. You will also be able to sell another 30 option contract against the stock. Albeit you will not get as much money for the 30 option now that the stock is at 28 as you did when the stock was at 30.

## The Option Contract

There are several terms that need to be defined before we can continue. They are the option price, the strike price, and expiration.

All options are contracts. There are three components to this contract.

- The agreed-upon price of the option
- The price at which the option may be exercised
- The duration of the option contract and its expiration date

1. All option contracts are for 100 shares of stock. The price of the option is multiplied times 100 per contract. This means that if the price of the option is $2.00 then one contract will cost $200.
2. The price at which the option may be exercised is called the strike price. If you sell an option with a $35 strike price, this means that you have agreed to sell your stock for $35 if it is called away by the purchaser of the option. The process of calling your stock away by the purchaser (requiring you to sell your stock) is known as exercising the option. You will then receive what is known as an assignment. You are assigned the sale of your stock at $35 per share.

   In order for this to happen, the stock must be greater than the strike price before the option expires. If the market value of the stock is not greater than the strike price then there would be no reason for the owner of the call option to want the stock at the strike price. If the market value of the stock is below the strike price then the call purchaser could simply go on the open market and buy it for less money.

In actuality you don't have to do anything. If you are assigned the sale of your stock, then your brokerage will simply sell it on your behalf. You will simply wake up one morning and see that your stock is gone and the money from the sale is in your account. If you did not have the stock in your account then it will still be sold, the proceeds placed in your account, and your account will show that you are *short* the stock. This means that you must eventually replace the stock you are short.

3. The last component of the contract is the duration of the option contract. This is quoted as a specific day rather than a time frame. Typically the standard monthly contract expires on the third Friday of any given month. (Technically it is the Saturday, but the markets are not open on Saturday.) Therefore a July 35 option on XYZ stock means that the option expires on the third Friday of July with a strike price of $35 per share of XYZ stock. The various strike prices and their expirations are set and fixed by the exchange.

## The Covered Call

What we have been describing so far is a covered call. This is the term used when you sell a call option on stock you already own. Therefore you are said to be covered by the stock.

It is possible to sell a call without owning the stock. If you do this you are said to be *naked* the call. This is probably one of the most dangerous things that you can do. As long as the price of the stock does not go up you are fine. The stock could go to zero and you still get to keep the option money from the sale of the call.

On the other hand if the stock goes up beyond the strike price then your stock will be called away. But you don't have any stock. Therefore when your stock is sold you will be short the stock and eventually you will be required to purchase the stock on the open market at a probable higher price to replace the stock that you are short. Obviously there is no limit to the loss that can be incurred.

Before you go out and start selling covered calls as a strategy it should be noted that even though if the stock goes up there is no risk of loss, only opportunity, there is risk of substantial loss on the downside. Although you are mitigating that loss with the sale of an option, your real risk for loss is the decline in the value of the stock.

## The Put Option

The put option gives the purchaser the right, not the obligation, to force the seller of the option to purchase his stock at a specified price during a specified time period.

What this means is that if you sell one July 30 put option on XYZ stock, any time prior to the third Friday of July you may be required to purchase from the owner of the put option 100 shares of XYZ stock at $30 per share regardless of its market value at the time.

If you purchase a July 30 put option on XYZ stock this gives you the right to force the seller of the put option to purchase your stock at $30 per share regardless of its market value at the time.

Why would you want to buy a put option? Let's say that you own 100 shares of XYZ stock which you purchased for $32 per share. Earnings on the stock are coming out in less than a month. You are afraid that if the earnings are bad it could devastate your stock. So you buy a put option that expires after the earnings announcement with a strike price of $30. If there are bad earnings and the price of the stock declines to $20 per share, you can force the seller of the put option to purchase your stock at $30 per share. Therefore your loss would only be $2 per share plus the price that you paid for the put option.

No matter how sure you are of your position Murphy is always alive and well. Something can go wrong. And sometimes it can be devastating. You never want to be in a position where if something devastating goes wrong you can lose a good portion of your entire account. Therefore savvy investors will always use some form of a hedge (protection) in order to limit the loss.

Most put options are purchased as hedges or insurance policies against major declines in stock positions. It is also possible to purchase put options as an alternate strategy to shorting stock in the belief that the stock will go down.

## Intrinsic and Extrinsic Values

The price of a call or put option is determined primarily by the laws of supply and demand. But the law of supply and demand only governs what is known as extrinsic or premium value.

Assume that XYZ stock is selling for $32 per share. A call option with a $30 strike price has a value of $2 intrinsically. What this means is that the owner of the call option can force the seller of the option to sell his stock to him for $30 per share. He can then immediately sell the stock for $32 per share on the open market. Therefore the option has a value of at least $2.00.

This is known as intrinsic value. You can always find what the intrinsic value of a call option is by subtracting the strike price of a call option from the market price if the market price is higher. In the case of a put option, subtract the strike price from the market price if the market price is lower. Ignore the minus sign. An option that has intrinsic value is said to be In the Money. An option that has no intrinsic value is said to be Out of the Money. If the market price of the stock is exactly the same as the strike price it is said to be At the Money.

If an option is selling for more than its intrinsic value then the difference between the intrinsic value and the price of the option is said to be its extrinsic value or premium value.

The price of options which are In the Money will be made up of two parts, intrinsic value and extrinsic value. The price of options which are Out of the Money or At the Money will be made up of only extrinsic value. The price of an option is affected by the price of the underlying stock. Assuming the same amount of time remains until expiration, as the price of the underlying stock goes up or down, the price of the option will also go up or down (although not necessarily at the same one to one ratio).

Let's assume that XYZ stock is selling for $30 per share. You have purchased a July 35 call option for $1. The next day the stock is selling for $32 per share. Because the stock is closer to the strike price at $32 per share than it was at $30 per share, the value of the call option should also increase. This is because it has a better chance at $32 of being In the Money by expiration than it had when the stock was at $30.

How much it will increase is for another discussion. The only thing that is important here is to understand that the $1.00 option that you purchased when the stock was selling for $30 is worth more now that the stock is selling for $32.

Let's assume now that the stock is selling for $36 per share. The 35 call option now has an intrinsic value of $1.00 per share plus whatever premium it may warrant for the time remaining until expiration. The premium (extrinsic) value is also known as time value because time is what you are really buying when you buy an option.

## Opening and Closing Contracts

Whenever you buy or sell an option for the first time you are said to be opening a contract. At any time until expiration you have the right to get out of that contract. This is called closing the contract.

In order to close an option contract you simply create an opposite transaction from what was used to open the contract.

For example: let's assume that you sold a July 30 call option for $2.00; and $200 was deposited to your account. Time goes by and the price of the stock has not moved. The July 30 call option is now valued at $1.25. It has decreased in value because there is now less time available. At this time you wish to get out or close the contract. Since you sold the option for $2.00 initially, all that you need to do now to close the contract is to buy an option with the same strike price and same expiration for $1.25. It does not have to be from the same person that bought your option. In fact you will never know who that person was.

All July 30 call options are equal and interchangeable. This means that all options of the same type (call or put), the same strike price, and the same expiration date are the same. When you buy back an option that you previously sold or sell an option that you previously bought, then you are closing the contract and have no further obligation. Whether you make money or lose money in the closed transaction is simply a matter of what you paid for the option versus what you sold it for. In the above example you sold the option for $2.00 and bought it back for $1.25. In this case you made $0.75 or $75 profit on one contract.

# Option Pricing

The pricing of an option is not an arbitrary endeavor. Options can be viewed as the market sentiment on the underlying stock. The more demand there is for an option, be it a put or call, the larger the value of the premium. The largest amount of premium is found with a strike price At the Money. As the strike price goes either further In the Money or Out of the Money the amount of premium on the option is reduced.

Another thing that affects the pricing of an option is how close it is to its expiration date. The premium on an option is reduced exponentially as the expiration date approaches. This makes logical sense. In reality, time is what the option purchaser is buying. This is known as time decay. But time does not decay the premium of an option at a constant rate. The closer an option is to expiration, time decay accelerates at an exponential rate.

# Delta

The Greeks are an aid to helping you understand how options are priced. They are Delta, Theta, Gamma, and Vega. These are terms (borrowed from the Greek alphabet) which are used to describe what is happening to the price of an option. For our purposes we are only interested in Delta and Theta. Every brokerage firm's option software will provide you with these values.

Delta is technically defined as the amount by which an option will increase or decrease in price if the underlying stock moves by $1.00.

But Delta is much more than that. Delta is actually your oddsmaker. If an option is absolutely At the Money it has a 50–50 chance statistically of expiring either In the Money or Out of the Money. Therefore an option whose strike price is At the Money has a Delta of 0.50.

Let's take a look at how this works. Assume the stock has a price of $100 and its option with a strike price of 100 has a Delta of 0.50. This actually means two things. First if the stock price increases to $101 the premium value of the 100 call option will increase by $0.50 (the percentage amount of the Delta). Of course the price will actually increase by $1.50 because it will now have $1.00 of intrinsic value plus the $0.50

of increase in premium value. If the price of the stock goes to $99 then the call option will lose $0.50 of premium value. The other meaning of a Delta of 0.50 is that there is a 50 percent chance that the 100 strike price option will be At or In the Money at expiration or a 50 percent chance that the 100 option will be Out of the Money at expiration.

For our purposes we are going to be using Delta as the oddsmaker. Other than At the Money which always has a Delta of 0.50, other things can affect the value of Delta. Delta can be affected by volatility.

You can think of volatility as a fear factor. Most investors in the market are mostly long the market, meaning that the purchaser or owner of stock is betting that the stock will go up. As the stock declines in price, fear sets in. The more the stock declines, the more fear there is. This fear is measured as volatility. The higher the volatility, the higher is the price of an option, especially a put option.

Volatility also affects what is known as the expected movement of the stock. This in turn affects the Delta of the option. Remember Delta is the oddsmaker. If the expected move of the stock increases then the odds that it will be In the Money or Out of the Money at expiration is affected.

## Theta

Theta is the measure of time decay. It is expressed as either a positive or negative number. For now, pay no attention to the + or − sign. A Theta of +0.45 and a Theta of −0.45 both mean that the option value itself will lose $0.45 per day.

The + or − sign refers to what you personally will gain or lose, not what the option value will gain or lose. Remember that as time passes all options will decay and lose value because of time.

If you are the purchaser of an option then you will have a negative Theta (meaning time decay will go against you). The call option you purchased will lose value as time gets closer to expiration.

If you are the seller of an option then you will have a positive Theta (meaning you will benefit from time decay). The reason a seller benefits from time decay is because the option has already been sold. Therefore it must be bought back at some time or left to expire. Therefore the seller wants the option to be at the lowest price possible when it is bought back or for it to expire worthless.

Theta does not stay constant. It is affected by the passage of time and by volatility. The closer you get to expiration the faster Theta will increase.

## Risk Graphs

The purpose of a risk graph is to graphically show you what your risk versus reward is. What it doesn't do is make a prediction as to where the stock is headed. Furthermore the main part of the risk graph is only valid at expiration.

Look at Figure 2.1 This is a risk graph of what is known as a bull spread. The price of the stock is the horizontal line at the bottom, and the profit loss is the vertical line on the left. As the stock is moving to the right, meaning increasing in price, the profit of the position also increases until such time as it reaches its maximum profit potential. At that point no matter how much higher the stock rises the profit is capped.

As the stock is moving to the left, meaning decreasing in price, the loss is also increasing until such time as it reaches its maximum loss. At that point, no matter how much lower the stock declines the loss is capped. You can also tell from this graph what the risk versus the reward is.

Figure 2.2 is a bear spread. As the stock is moving to the left, meaning decreasing in price, the profit of the position also increases until such time

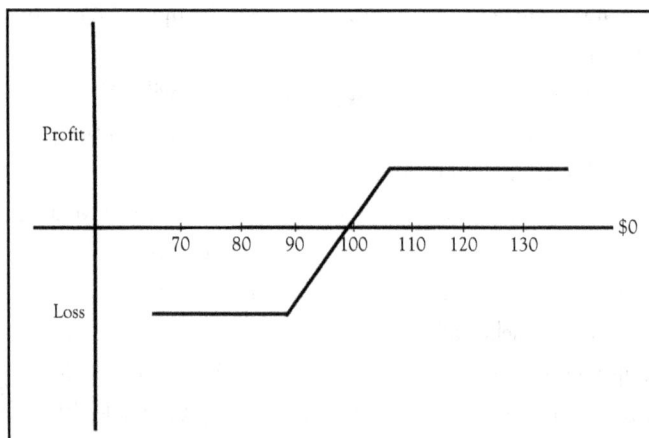

Figure 2.1 Bull spread

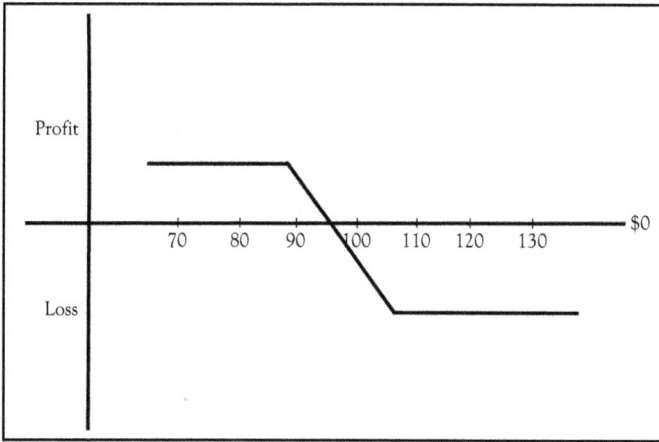

**Figure 2.2  Bear spread**

as it reaches its maximum profit potential. At that point, no matter how much lower the stock declines the profit is capped.

As the stock is moving to the right meaning increasing in price the loss of the position is also increasing until such time as it reaches its maximum loss. At that point no matter how much higher the stock goes the loss is capped.

Figure 2.3 is simply a risk graph of a long stock purchase. This means you have simply purchased the stock. As the stock moves to the right and increases in price the profit increases and is never capped. The potential gain is unlimited.

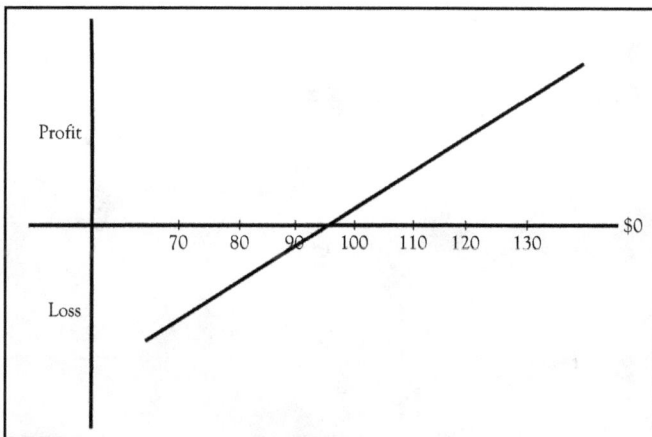

**Figure 2.3  Long stock**

On the other hand as the stock moves to the left and declines in price the potential loss increases and can be absolute and total.

A risk graph can be created with most brokerage platforms using any combination of options and stock. We will be looking at a risk graph for many of the basic strategies that we cover.

# CHAPTER 3

# Basic Stock and Option Strategies

## The Risky Stock Trade

Buying stock is an easy investment to make. And this is what most people do. You simply buy a stock, hope that it goes up, then sell it. What could be simpler?

The problem with this kind of trade is that it can be very risky. Stocks go down as well as up. Although theoretically there is no limit to the upside potential, you can also have a total loss of capital.

Go back and look at the risk graph for a long stock purchase in Figure 2.3.

### What Is the Risk?

Believe it or not, this can be one of the riskiest trades that you can make. There is absolutely no protection to the downside. You might say though that you haven't really lost anything if you do not sell the stock. You've simply incurred a paper loss. The problem with this theory is that you're assuming that the stock will come back at least to where you bought it.

You might think that this kind of risk only happens with risky or speculative companies. You might have the assumption that if you invest in good solid companies paying good dividends, this couldn't happen to you. Believe me. Anything can happen. Look what happened to General Motors.

What's good for General Motors is good for the United States. Even though General Motors exists today it is not the same company. Those that owned common stock in the original General Motors took a beating. It never came back. And it paid a good dividend.

### Can a Stock Really Go to Zero?

Can a stock really go to zero? You bet it can. Think Enron, Lehman Brothers, General Motors, the dot-coms of the early 2000s, all of the airlines that don't exist now such as Braniff, Pan Am, and Eastern Airlines. And those were the big companies. And it doesn't take much research to find speculative high-flying companies that were the darlings of the time that are no longer with us.

Simply stated, buying or selling stock without any kind of protection incurs an absolute and total risk.

### How Can You Protect Yourself?

When you buy stock there are ways that you can protect yourself from a total downside risk.

#### Stop Orders

The stop order is the most common form of protection from downside risk that most people use. It is rather simple to implement.

Simply decide how much you are willing to risk and place an order with your broker that if the price of the stock falls to that level, sell. The question is what kind of stop order are you going to put in place? There are basically two types: limit stop orders and market stop orders.

The limit stop order tells the brokerage firm that when the price of the stock reaches a certain price, place a limit order to sell the stock at a specified price. A limit order means that you are limiting the price at which you will sell the stock to the limit price or higher. If you cannot sell at that price or better, then do not execute the order. The problem with this type of order is that the price of the stock may be moving downward so fast that your limit order is not executed. This is especially true if it gapped down below your limit order at the market open. At that point the stop has failed.

The market stop order tells the brokerage firm that when the price of the stock reaches a certain price, place a market order to sell the stock.

A market order tells your broker to sell the stock at the prevailing market price whatever that is at the time. You are absolutely guaranteed to sell your stock. This will work. This will get you out of the stock, but you have no guarantee as to the price.

Let's assume that you bought a stock at $100 per share. You place a market stop order at $97 per share. Therefore you assume that your risk is limited to $3.00 per share. You look at your computer the next morning and see that the bid–ask on the stock has gapped down to $85 per share. That is where the stock will open the next day. Your market order is executed and you are out at $85 per share. Your loss is now $15 instead of $3.00. Even though technically the stop order worked, it didn't work as you had expected. And you will feel bad if, after catching your stock at $85 for a $15 loss, the stock then goes back up.

## Trailing Stops

The trailing stop is not designed to protect you from a loss, but to protect your profit. Let's assume that you purchased the stock at $100 per share. The stock has now risen to $120 per share. You have a nice $20 per share profit. You could sell at this point, but you think that the stock could go higher. You don't want to take the risk that it could return to $100 per share and that you would lose all that profit. Or even worse the price could go below $100 per share and you could incur a loss.

The trailing stop is designed to lock in a profit and, at the same time, to give you the potential to stay in the market for an even larger profit.

Let's assume that you want to place a $2.00 trailing stop. What this means is that initially with the stock at $120 per share, if the stock drops to $118 per share the stock is then sold. As the stock rises the stop order automatically trails the stock by $2.00 from its highest price. Therefore if the stock rises to $125 per share you are stopped out if it declines to $123 per share.

Here you have the same problem that you had with a regular stop order. You have to decide whether your trailing stop is going to be a limit trailing stop or a market trailing stop.

## Protective Puts

Protective puts offer a guaranteed protection. Let's assume that you purchased the stock at $92 per share. A 2½-month put with a strike price of 90 is purchased for $3.50. Very disappointing earnings come out, and the stock plummets to $80 per share. The put provided you with absolute protection at $90 per share because you can require the seller of the put to purchase your shares at $90. Therefore you have a $5.50 loss ($2.00 loss on the sale of the stock at $90 and $3.50 loss on the purchase of the put).

The put gave you an absolute protection at $90 per share plus the cost of the put, whereas with a stop order we have seen that there is no absolute protection. With a stop order there is no guarantee that you will exit the trade with a limit stop order or that you can control the market price with a market stop order.

There is one major problem with protective puts. They are extremely expensive. The protective put is a viable alternative for very short-term protection. If earnings are coming out in a couple of weeks and you wish to protect your position from what might be an explosive surprise to the downside, a protective put can be very effective.

On the other hand, to buy a one-year 90 strike price put on the same stock would cost you about $7.00. If you bought the 2½- to 3-month shorter-term protection throughout the year you could spend as much as $17 on the puts. This can become very expensive on a stock that may not move more than 10 percent per year.

So as you can see for a short-term protection the protective put is a viable alternative. But as you will see there is a better and less expensive way to protect your stock.

## Collar

The collar is a method of adding protection to a stock that you already own. It consists of selling an Out of the Money call and buying an Out of the Money put in the same expiration month. You generally want the price of the call that you sell to be priced higher than the put that you buy. If the options expire without the stock moving then you should at least break even on your transaction costs. You make money when the stock goes up toward the strike price of the call that you sold, and you are protected if the stock goes down.

Let's assume that you bought a stock for $92 per share. In order to protect that stock you sold a 30-day 95 call for $1.55. You bought an 88 put for $1.25. This gives you a $0.30 credit on the transaction. The maximum profit that you can make is $330 ($3.00 per share if the stock reaches $95 at expiration, $1.55 on the call that you sold which is being exercised by the purchaser, and you lose $1.25 on the now worthless put that you purchased; 3.00 + 1.55–1.25 = 3.30).

If the stock goes below $88 per share the most that you can lose is $370. (You will lose $4.00 per share on the stock. You will exercise your put and force the seller of the put to purchase your stock at $88 per share. You paid $92. The call that you sold is now worthless and you collect $1.55. You lose $1.25 on the put that you purchased. Therefore it is –$4.00 + $1.55 – $1.25 = $3.70 loss.)

As you will notice when we later talk about spreads, the collar as described above is nothing more than a synthetic bull spread with a maximum gain of $330 and a maximum loss of $370. A collar as described above should only be used to protect stock that you already own. A bull spread is much more economical and has less transaction costs as a strategy. (A synthetic is a combination of options and/or stock that has the exact or nearly exact risk graph as another option or stock strategy.)

Doubling Down—Are You Crazy?

One of the quickest ways to the poor house is through a strategy of doubling down as the price falls. This is not to be confused with a tried and true method of accumulation.

Let's assume a stock is selling for $65 per share. Your goal is to purchase 300 shares. Instead of purchasing all 300 shares at $65 per share, you purchase 100 shares at $65 per share. If the stock drops to $62 per share you purchase another 100 shares. And if the stock drops to $59 per share you purchase your final 100 shares. This is known as dollar cost averaging. Your average cost of the stock is $62 instead of $65 per share.

Here is another way you could dollar cost average. After you purchase your first 100 shares at $65 per share, immediately sell a 62 put naked. Normally you would not sell naked puts because you could be forced to purchase the stock at the strike price if the stock declines. But in this case that is your goal. You want to be able to purchase the stock at $62 per share. But the problem is the stock may never reach $62 per share. If it doesn't, wouldn't it be nice to have the premium from the sale of the put?

In this case you are going to sell a 62 put for $1.20. Here we are looking at 30-day options. You may choose any time frame that you think is appropriate. You also could sell at this time the 59 put for approximately $0.60. Or you can wait until the stock is lower in order to sell the 59 put. In any event if the stock never reaches $62 per share you have the consolation of pocketing at least $120 per 100 shares for the sale of the put. If at expiration the stock is less than $62 per share you will be forced to purchase the stock at $62 per share which was your goal in the first place. In any event you still get to keep the $1.20.

This is not the strategy that I am referring to when I talk about doubling down. Although dollar cost averaging can still result in a loss, you're still in better shape than if you had purchased all 300 shares at $65 per share and the stock declined.

Doubling down is a strategy in order to protect you from a loss. That is, every time a stock drops a given amount you simply purchase more stock. The theory is that eventually the stock will come back up and by purchasing more and more stock on the way down you have lowered your average cost of the stock which gives you a lower price for breakeven.

Unfortunately this comes under the trying to catch a falling knife theory. It has two assumptions. The first assumption is that there is a bottom. The second assumption is that the stock will come back. There is a third assumption. The stock will come back before you give out of money. And this can totally wipe you out especially if you are doing it on margin.

## Covered Calls

The covered call has been talked about previously. It is the purchase of stock and at the same time selling an Out of the Money call.

Normally the sale of a call by itself is considered to be a naked call. If exercised the seller of the call is required to deliver the stock to the purchaser of the call at the strike price. It is considered naked because the potential loss is unlimited since the seller of a call does not currently own the stock to be delivered.

If the seller of the call does not currently own the stock it must be purchased on the open market at the prevailing price in order for it to be delivered to the purchaser of a call if the call is exercised. On the other hand if the seller of the call already owns the stock, and the call is exercised, then the stock is simply sold and delivered, and there is no further obligation. Therefore the call is said to be covered by the stock.

### What Are the Risks?

At first glance it would seem that the covered call is a very safe investment. After all if the stock doesn't move you simply keep the premium from the sale of the call. If the stock goes up you get the appreciation from the sale of the stock at a higher price as well as getting to keep the premium from the sale of the call.

You are even protected somewhat on the downside by the reduction in the cost of the stock through the premium gained from the sale of the call. Then it would seem that the risk is really only in the lost opportunity for a larger gain if the stock goes up.

Look at the risk graph in Figure 3.1 for a covered call. Notice that the downside risk is total and absolute while the upside gain is capped. Notice also that the risk graph takes into consideration the premium received on the call as simply a reduction in the cost of the stock.

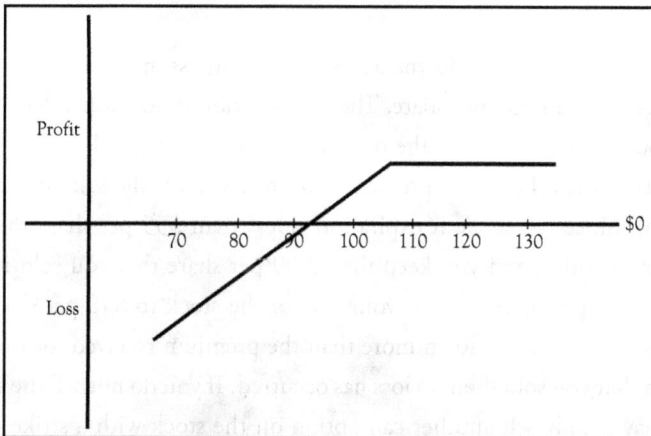

*Figure 3.1 Covered call*

## Upside Risk

Let's assume you purchased a stock for $50 per share. You sell a 30-day option on the stock with a strike price of $55 for $2.00 per share. Unless the option contract is closed that $2.00 per share is yours to keep no matter what.

At expiration if the price of the stock is equal to or less than $55 per share, the call option that you sold expires worthless and you keep the entire $2.00. You also keep your stock, and you are now permitted to sell another call option.

At expiration assume the price of the stock is greater than $55 per share (it really doesn't matter how high the stock goes). You are now required to sell and deliver the stock to the purchaser of the call. You have made a total of $7.00 per share. Since the stock price is above $55 per share you are required to sell the purchaser of the call your stock for $55. Therefore you made $5.00 per share on the sale of stock. Since you get to keep all of the premium from the sale of the call, you now made an additional $2.00 for a total of $7.00 per share profit.

The problem is that if the stock is $60 at expiration you must sell your stock at $55. As such you have missed out on five additional dollars of appreciation of the stock. This should be seen simply as lost opportunity since there is no actual financial loss.

## Downside Risk

Your real risk is on the downside. At expiration assume the price of the stock is less than $50 per share. The real question is how much less.

Your breakeven cost on the transaction is now $48 per share ($50 cost of stock minus the $2.00 premium you received on the sale of the call option). Since the stock at expiration is less than $55 per share the call expires worthless and you keep the $2.00 per share that you sold it for. That $2.00 per share reduces your cost of the stock to $48 per share. If the stock does not go down more than the premium received for the call option that you sold then no loss has occurred. If you do not sell the stock you may simply sell another call option on the stock with a strike price of $48 or higher and be guaranteed a profit assuming there is no further decline in the stock beyond the new premium that you have received.

On the other hand the loss can be substantial depending on how far down the stock declines. Let's assume at expiration the stock has gone down $10 instead of going up $10. The stock is now selling for $40 per share. If you sell the stock at this point your loss is $8.00 per share. You bought the stock for $50 per share and sold the stock for $40 per share incurring a $10 loss minus the $2.00 that you received from the sale of the option, thus creating the $800 loss on 100 shares.

As the stock is declining what is happening to the value of the call option. It is also declining. Depending upon how much time remains on the contract, when the stock reaches $48 the option might be valued at $0.50. But the problem is that you cannot sell the stock while the call option is still open. If you were to sell the stock without closing the call option you would now create a naked call situation, meaning that the call is no longer covered as you no longer own the stock.

Therefore the only way to sell the stock is to also close the option. Since the call option is now selling for $0.50 you therefore have made a $1.50 on the option transaction, but you have lost $2.00 on the stock transaction for a loss of $0.50.

If the stock continues to decline there will come a point that the value of the call option will be nearly worthless and can be purchased back and closed for as little as $0.05. But that will probably occur when the stock is substantially below your breakeven point.

Therefore using the covered call as a strategy can be almost as risky as simply owning and holding stock. This is not to say that a covered call strategy should never be used. It could be used as a strategy that you might want to incorporate with a stock that you are determined to hold no matter what. If that is the case you might say to yourself why not create a little extra income while I'm holding the stock.

Remember that if this is the case and the stock appreciates substantially during the time that you have a call written against it, you may be forced to sell the stock and then buy it back later at a higher price in order to maintain your position.

### Can a Losing Covered Call Be Fixed?

Most of the time when we talk about fixing a covered call position, we are referring to trying to salvage a substantially losing trade. In the above example where the stock was purchased at $50 per share and has now declined to $40 per share, what can be done to mitigate your loss? There are several possibilities and here are two of the most common.

## Rolling Down

In all of the strategies to fix a covered call, time is your main variable. It depends on how far in the contract timewise you are when the precipitous drop in the value of the stock occurred. The earlier it occurs the more time value you have to work with in order to attempt to fix it.

The other variable is how far down the stock has declined before you attempted to fix it. For example it is much easier to attempt to fix it when the stock has declined to $45 than it is when the stock has declined to $40.

Rolling down means that you close the call option that you sold and simultaneously sell another call option with the same expiration at a lower strike price. Here is an example.

You purchased the stock for $50 and sold a 30-day call option with a strike price of $55 for $2.00. Two days later the stock has dropped to $45 per share. Your breakeven cost at this point is $48 per share. With the stock at $45 the call option that you sold is now valued at $0.50. Your strategy is to roll down. Buy back the 55 call option for $0.50 and sell the 50 call option for $2.00. You have now brought in $3.50, $1.50 profit on the 55 call option and $2.00 on the sale of the 50 call option. Your breakeven cost now is $46.50. Now as long as the stock at expiration is $46.50 or greater you will not have lost any money.

Assume that the decline in the stock is relentless. A week later it falls to $40. You attempt to do another roll down. You see that the 50 call option is now virtually worthless, and you buy it back for $0.05. Your breakeven cost is $46.55. There are now less than 2½ weeks on the contract. Your next available strike price is $45. The price of that option is only $0.75. You decide to go ahead and sell the call option. Now no matter what happens to the stock you have locked in a loss.

Here is your situation. You have now put yourself in a situation where you are required to determine the direction of the stock over the next 2 weeks. Your breakeven cost is $45.80 ($46.55–$0.75). If the stock rallies to above $45 per share you will be required to sell the stock at $45 and incur a $0.80 loss. At expiration if the stock is greater than $40 and less than $45 you can probably sell another one-month 45 for $2.00 and further reduce your cost.

On the other hand if the stock continues to decline it will become more and more difficult to roll down without locking in substantial losses. With the stock at $35 you could be forced to sell a 40 or even a 37.50 in order to get any decent premium at all with a breakeven price above 40. You will probably be okay if the price stabilizes for a period of time, but if it continues to drop you could be in real trouble.

Even though a stock drop of this magnitude creates an inevitable loss, it doesn't mean that if you are caught in this situation you should not attempt a roll down. Let's assume that your final roll down was at $37.50. And the stock rallies to 38. Your breakeven cost we will assume is $42 because of the various roll downs. You have now lost $4.50 plus transaction costs.

But where would you be if you had not attempted to fix your situation through the use of roll downs? After your first initial sale of a call option for $2.00 with a strike price of 55 your breakeven cost was $48. If you had chosen to do nothing with the stock at 38, the loss would be $10 per share instead of $4.50.

## More Time

Earlier I said that time was a major variable. Depending on how much time remains on the contract and how far the stock has declined, there may not be enough premium available at a reasonable strike price without locking in a substantial loss.

Let's assume that with the stock at $40 per share your breakeven cost is at $46.55. You are not prepared to lock in a loss at this point. If you sell the current expiration month 45 call for $0.75 your breakeven price will be $45.80 thus locking in a $0.80 loss if the stock rallies above $45 per share. You will also have very little protection if the stock continues to drop.

Remember that the price of an option is determined not only by how far In or Out of the Money the option is, but also by how much time remains on the option contract until expiration. Even though the current month option with less than 2½ weeks remaining is selling for $0.75, you see that a three-month option with a strike price of 45 is selling for $2.50. In essence you decide to do a combination of a roll down to 45 as well as sell the three-month option. Your new breakeven is $44.05. Therefore you have not only not locked in a loss, but if the stock rallies above $45 in the next three months at expiration you actually will have a small profit minus transaction costs. Furthermore you have reduced your breakeven cost by another $2.50 which will give you a little more protection if the stock continues to decline.

As with the simple roll down there will come a point that no matter how far out you go into the future with your expiration you will not be able to avoid the possibility of locking in a loss.

## Buying Long Calls

Buying a single call anywhere within the option chain is simple and easy. What is difficult is choosing the right strike price and the right expiration time frame.

Look at Figure 3.2, the long call. As you can see from the risk graph the long call has unlimited profit potential. At the same time it has a limited risk. But the risk graph does not tell the whole story.

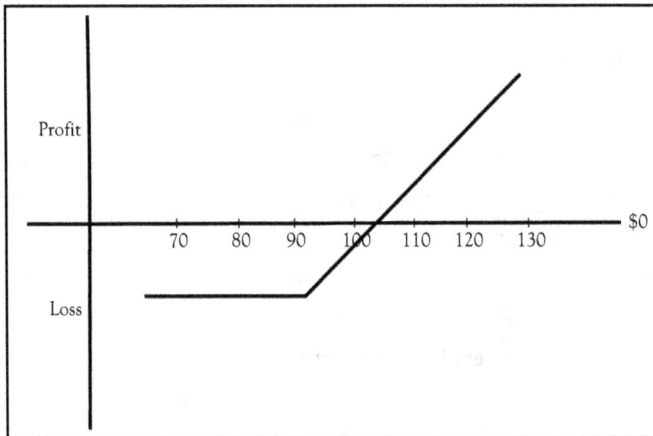

Figure 3.2  The long call

The second you buy a call Theta is working against you. What this means is that every day that passes the call will lose value.

The first decision that has to be made is at what strike price you are going to purchase. The further Out of the Money that you go the cheaper the call. Looking at the Delta for the calls, you choose one that looks inexpensive and has a 0.30 Delta. This means two things. For every $1.00 that the underlying stock moves, the option premium will move by $0.30. It also means that it has a 30 percent chance of being In the Money at expiration. The flip side of that is there is a 70 percent chance that you will lose your entire investment if you hold it until expiration. Are these really good odds?

Also by purchasing Out of the Money calls you are subject to what is known as the Volatility Paradox. Remember as volatility increases the price of an option at a given strike price also increases. As volatility decreases the price of that same option decreases. If you are purchasing an option after a sustained downturn, chances are volatility is very high and is reflected in the price of the option which is going to be very expensive. Let's assume that the stock then turns around and goes in your favor. Now that the stock is moving up volatility is decreasing. As volatility decreases the premium value of your option also decreases. You can find yourself in the unfortunate situation of having been correct in the direction of the stock and the timing and still either lose money on the call option or not make nearly as much profit as you thought you were going to.

Let's see what it's going to take to make money with a call option. Let's assume the stock is selling for $50 per share. You purchase a one-month 55 call option for $2.00. If the stock moves immediately upward toward the $55 strike price the value of the $2.00 option will increase according to its Delta. For example, if the stock has a 0.35 Delta then for every $1.00 movement in the stock price the option will move $0.35. Let's assume the stock gained $3.00 the day after you bought the option. Then the option should be selling around $3.05. That's a $105.00 profit on a $200 investment. Not bad!

The problem here is that the stock had to move almost immediately after you purchased the option before Theta had a chance to rear its ugly head.

Let's assume that this is a very slow moving stock, but it is going in the right direction. On or around expiration date it has finally moved above

$55 per share. Along the way Theta has eaten away a lot of the premium as time went by as well as being the victim of the Volatility Paradox. Since most of the time premium has evaporated what you're left with is simply intrinsic value in order to make a profit. This means that your breakeven cost is $57 per share on the stock. At $57 per share there is a $2.00 intrinsic value which is what you paid for the option. This means that the stock at expiration must be above $57 per share for you to make a penny.

Let's go back and look at Delta again. What we see is that when you purchased the option the 55s had a Delta of 0.35. But remember your breakeven is not $55 on the stock. Your breakeven at expiration is $57 on the stock. Look at the Delta for the 57. It's sitting at 0.21. This gets worse and worse. That means you only have a 21 percent chance of making one penny if the option goes to expiration. It also means that you have a 79 percent chance that the best you will do is break even or lose your entire investment. Those odds are horrible. It is no wonder that the purchaser of calls almost always loses money.

## Buying Long Puts

Buying a long put has all the same hazards and risks as buying long calls. Look at Figure 3.3, the long put. Notice it is the same as the long call except in the opposite direction. Here you are hoping that the stock is going down instead of going up.

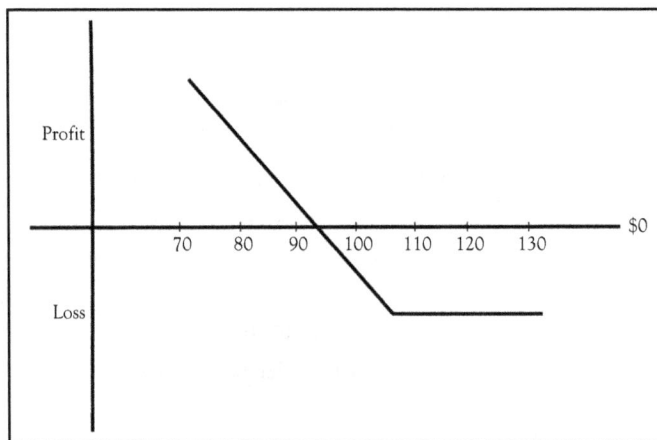

Figure 3.3  The long put

If you are bearish on the stock many times buying a put is a lot easier than shorting the stock and uses a lot less capital. The advantage of using a put over shorting the stock is that you are at least limiting your risk.

Generally puts are more expensive than calls. The reason for this is that puts are also used as insurance in order to protect a portfolio. As such they are in more demand than calls. Anything that has a high demand generally is more expensive.

Assuming that the stock goes in the correct direction (down), it is easier to make money with a put than it is with a call. The reason is that as a stock declines volatility increases. The Volatility Paradox is working now in your favor. If the stock had had a previously high run-up then volatility should have been at a low level. As such the cost of a put is less expensive. As the stock goes down volatility increases and so does the premium on the put. This works in your favor as you will eventually sell the put at a higher price.

At the same time you still have that Theta and Delta problem. If the stock does not move in your direction quickly Theta will begin eating away at the time premium of your option. And if the option that you have purchased has a –0.35 Delta (puts are always expressed using a minus Delta but it means the same thing), this means that the option has only a 35 percent chance of being In the Money at expiration. You have a 65 percent chance of incurring a loss if held until expiration.

## Selling Naked Puts

Selling a naked put is a valid and useful strategy if you wish to accumulate stock. It starts with the assumption that you want to purchase the stock anyway. Since the reason you're using the naked put is to accumulate stock there is no reason for a risk graph.

Let's assume that a stock is selling for $63 per share. The stock has already had a little run-up and you think that it's due for a small pullback before it continues its upward climb. You really would like to purchase the stock for $60 per share. If the stock comes back to 60 then you will purchase 100 shares.

Let's make a little money along the way. You see that the 30-day 60 put is selling for $3.00 per share. Therefore you sell one contract and pocket $300. If at expiration the stock is selling for less than $60 per share you will be assigned and forced to buy the stock at 60 which is where you wanted to buy the stock to begin with. Not only do you have your stock at $60 per share, you also have an extra $3.00 per share on the sale of the option. If at expiration the stock is selling above $60 per share you keep the $300. In either event you keep the $300.

The problem with the strategy is that if you really want the stock at $60 per share you do not get to control when the put is exercised. As a result during the month the stock could come down to $60 per share where you wanted to buy it and then go back up. Then at expiration it may be at $68. At this point you would have missed out on purchasing the stock at $60 and only have the $300 as a consolation.

## Spreads and Custom Combos

An option spread or custom combo is simply the purchase and/or sale of two or more options. It is generally done to limit the risk inherent in buying and selling single options.

The spread is the buying of one strike and selling a different strike price of the same type and at the same expiration. Spreads may be created using calls or puts. It doesn't matter which strikes are purchased or which strikes are sold in order to constitute a spread.

If the spread is created using calls it is a call spread. If the spread is created using puts it is a put spread.

Virtually any strategy using more than one option will generally involve a spread of some sort. In fact even the most complicated option strategy can be broken down into a series of spreads.

A custom combo is simply the putting together in various combinations and quantities of more than one option in order to form a strategy.

### Credit Spreads

A credit spread is a spread where you receive money instead of costing you money. With puts it generally involves selling the higher strike price and buying the lower strike price. With calls it involves selling the lower strike price and buying the higher strike price. This results in a credit instead of a debit where you receive money into your account. Do not be misled. Just because you are receiving a credit into your account does not mean that the risk does not exceed the credit by a substantial amount.

Credit Call Spreads

Let's take a look at the credit call spread. We're obviously going to create this spread using calls. The credit call spread is a bearish spread. This means you make money when the underlying stock goes down instead of up. You lose money if the underlying stock goes up by more than the short (the one you sold) strike option.

Here is an example. Let's assume the underlying stock is selling for $50 per share. You create a 55/60 call spread by selling the 55 and buying the 60 strike. The 55 is selling for $2.00 and the 60 is selling for $0.80. This results in a net credit of $1.20.

Look at the risk graph in Figure 3.4. Notice that in a credit spread there is limited risk on the downside but also your profit is capped.

In this particular example it is a $5 spread. That is because there is a $5.00 difference between the two strike prices of the spread. This means at expiration the entire spread cannot be worth more than $5.00 no matter how high or how low the underlying stock goes. In order to compute your potential gain simply look at the credit received. You can never make

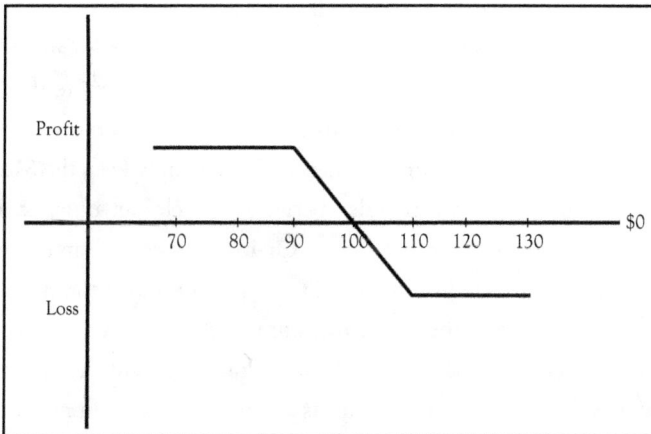

*Figure 3.4  Credit call spread*

more than the amount of the credit. But you can definitely lose more than the amount of the credit.

Your potential risk is computed by taking the maximum value of the spread which in this case is $5.00 and subtracting the credit received which in this case is $1.20. Therefore the most that you can lose no matter what happens in the spread is $3.80 (i.e., $5.00 – $1.20).

Let's look at how you make money with a credit call spread. Remember the underlying stock is currently selling for $50 per share. You have sold the 55 call. At expiration as long as the stock is below $55 per share both the 55 call that you sold and the 60 call that you bought will expire worthless. In that case you simply keep the entire $1.20 that you received initially as a credit. That is your profit.

The credit call spread is considered to be a bear spread because you make money if the stock goes down or for that matter it can go up as long as by expiration it does not reach the strike price of the option that you sold.

Let's see how you compute where your breakeven point will be. Simply add $1.20 to the $55 call that you sold. In this case your breakeven point is $56.20. If at expiration the stock is selling for more than $55 but is equal to or less than $56.20 then you will either make nothing or you will make a small amount.

Let's assume at expiration the stock is selling for $56. Your long 60 call option will expire worthless. The 55 call option is now worth $1.00. But you received $1.20. Therefore you will make $0.20.

Let's assume the stock drops $20 per share. You don't really care. All you care about is that at expiration the stock is not selling for more than $55 per share. What happens on the downside is irrelevant to you since at expiration both options will expire worthless and you simply keep the $1.20.

Credit call spreads are popular because a stock can only do three things. It can go up. It can go down. Or it can stay the same. That is the universe. With a credit call spread you make money if the stock goes down or the stock stays the same. You still make money even if the stock goes up but does not reach the short strike price beyond the credit that you received. It would seem that this is a neutral trade meaning that you do not care about trying to predict the direction of the underlying stock. But this is not really true. The credit call spread simply gives you a little bit of cushion and an edge. You still have to decide whether you think the stock will be going up or not. The difference is you are simply trying to predict the magnitude of an up move.

What are your chances of making money on a credit call spread? Let's assume you are the purchaser of the 55 call. What are your odds of making money? Look at the Delta. Let's assume the Delta is 0.35. What this means as the call purchaser is that at expiration there is a 35 percent chance that the underlying stock will be $55.01 or more. But this also means that the purchaser of the 55 call has a 65 percent chance that at expiration the call will expire worthless.

Therefore the credit call spread has a 65 percent chance of making money if held until expiration. It also has only a 35 percent chance of losing money. The odds are definitely in your favor. Or are they?

I have heard it said many times and read in many books that being the seller of options instead of the buyer of options is similar to a casino, but in this case the seller of the option is the house. I question whether this is really true. In a casino the house does not really care if you win or lose. Their only concern is that enough people are playing. The house makes money in the aggregate because it knows that the law of large numbers will produce the odds in the house's favor over the long run. Let's see if this is true in the credit call spread.

In the example given you will make $1.20, 65 out of 100 times that you create this credit call spread. You will lose $3.80, 35 out of 100 times. (This does not take into consideration the number of times that you do not make the full amount or lose the full amount.)

Let's do the math. Assume the spread is put on 100 times. $1.20 × 65 × 100 shares per contract equals $7,800. $3.80 × 35 × 100 shares per contract equals $13,300. This means that in the long run without any other directional information and without closing your trade before expiration, you will lose $5,500 on this trade.

I'm not trying to say by this example that you should not do credit call spreads. There are very good, risk-limited, option strategies that use credit spreads. And they are certainly better than simply buying single calls. The odds are definitely in your favor over simply purchasing the calls. And by not letting the spread go to expiration and using other mitigating techniques, you can make credit spreads work in your favor.

What I am saying is that you should not simply assume that because the odds are in your favor you can blindly sell credit call spreads and make money in the long run. You need to have other directional information or use the spread as a component of an overall strategy.

## Credit Put Spreads

The credit put spread is opposite of the credit call spread. You are obviously now using puts instead of calls. The credit put spread is a bullish spread. That is to say you make money when the stock either stays the same or goes up. You lose money if the stock goes down by more than the short strike price.

The credit put spread is created by selling a put with the higher strike price and buying a lower strike price. Let's look at an example.

Let's assume the stock is selling for $50 per share. You're going to create a 45/40 credit put spread. You sell the 45 put and buy the 40 put.

Let's assume in this example that you receive a $1.80 credit. The credit put spread mathematically works the same as the credit call spread. The distance of the spread is $5.00. Again that is the maximum that the spread is worth no matter what happens to the underlying stock. Therefore the most that you can make is the amount of the credit received

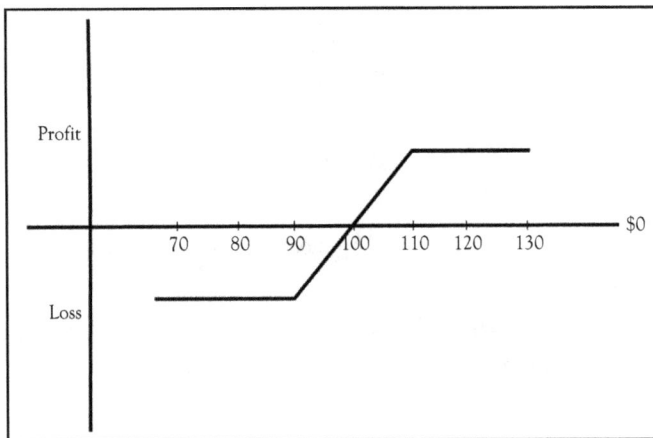

*Figure 3.5 Credit put spread*

which is $1.80. Subtract $1.80 from the $5.00 spread and the most that you can lose is $3.20. To compute your breakeven point subtract the premium received from the short strike price. In this case the short strike is $45. The premium is $1.80. Therefore your breakeven price for the stock is $43.20. As long as the stock stays equal to or above $43.20 you will either breakeven or make money.

Look at the risk of graph in Figure 3.5. Notice that it is the mirror image of the credit call spread. You have both limited risk and limited profit. You make money if the stock stays the same or goes up. You lose money if the stock goes down.

With the credit put spread you can also compute your odds of making money by looking at the Delta. You use the same calculations even though the Delta is expressed as a negative number. Simply ignore the minus sign.

### Ratio Spreads

Normally a spread uses equal numbers of calls for a credit call spread or puts for a credit put spread. But it is also possible to sell and buy more of one strike price than another.

Let's assume on the credit call spread that you sell two 55s and buy one 60. Be careful here because you have one naked call. This can be broken down into one credit call spread plus one naked call.

What we are creating here is known as a ratio spread, because the two strike prices in the spread differ by a ratio. What that ratio is, is up to you. Let's assume that we reverse it. We will sell one 55 and we will buy two 60s. In this case it might continue as a credit spread where we receive money or depending upon the price of the two 60s that we buy it may turn into a debit spread where it costs us money. In any case we will lose money if the stock at expiration is more than 55 and less than 60. As the stock goes beyond $60 we will begin to overtake the loss on the 55 which is maxed out at a given amount, and we will begin to make money depending on how far above 60 the stock goes.

Any combination of a ratio spread can be created depending on what your feelings are about the direction of the stock.

### Debit Spreads

A debit spread is the opposite of a credit spread in that you pay money instead of receiving money. Generally speaking, with a debit spread you can only lose the amount of money paid for the spread. The amount of the debit is your risk.

A debit spread is a little more logical and easier to understand than credit spreads. If you are long a debit call spread you make money when the stock goes up. If you are long a debit put spread you make money when the stock goes down.

### Debit Call Spreads

The debit call spread has the same risk graph as the credit put spread; that is, it is a bullish trade. Your risk is limited to the cost of the spread on the downside, and your profit is limited to the distance of the spread minus the cost of the spread.

Here is how a debit call spread is constructed. Let's assume that the stock is selling for $50 per share. You purchase a 50/55 call spread. Buy the 50 strike and sell the 55 strike. Let's assume that the cost of the spread is $2.25. The value of the entire spread is $5. This is the distance between 50 and 55. This is the most money that you can receive when the spread is sold. Therefore your maximum profit is the $5.00 value of the spread minus the $2.25 that you paid for the spread. Therefore the most that you can make is $2.75.

### Debit Put Spreads

The debit put spread has the same risk graph as the credit call spread; that is, it is a bearish trade. Your risk is limited to the cost of the spread on the downside, and your profit is limited to the distance of the spread minus the cost of the spread.

Here is how a debit put spread is constructed. Let's assume that the stock is selling for $50 per share. You purchase a 50/45 put spread. Buy the 50 strike and sell the 45 strike. Let's assume that the cost of the spread is $1.75. The value of the entire spread is $5.00. This is the distance between 50 and 45. This is the most money that you can receive when the spread is sold. Therefore your maximum profit is the $5.00 value of the spread minus the $1.75 that you paid for the spread. Thus the most that you can make is $3.25.

### High-Probability Credit Spreads

The concept behind the high-probability credit spread is that you can create an income stream by selling far out of the money credit spreads, either put credit spreads or call credit spreads. The rationale is that if you go far enough out of the money in the shortest period of time the credit spreads will simply expire worthless and you will get to keep the entire premium that you received.

What you have to understand is that the option market is very efficient. If it were that easy everyone would be doing it. The problem is you have two things working against you, Delta and volatility. You don't really have to worry about the volatility because it will take care of itself since it is already reflected in the Delta and the price of the option spread. But be aware volatility is affecting Delta.

How Far Out of the Money?

It doesn't matter how far out of the money you go. The efficiency of the option market is already working against you. For example, I am looking at the SPY for an eight-day call option with a 0.09 Delta. This is a $2.00 spread. If I sold this I would receive $0.13. In order to make it worth my while I will sell 10 of them. This will bring in $130. The chance that I will get to keep the entire $130 is 91 percent. That's pretty good. This means that there is only a 9 percent chance that I will begin to lose some money. Remember that you begin your losses at the lower strike price (short strike) of the spread. Your maximum loss comes at the higher strike price (long strike) of the spread. Now look at the Delta of the higher strike. I see that its Delta is 0.05. This means that 5 percent of the time I will lose the entire $1,870 if taken to expiration.

Remember this is a $2.00 spread and I am only receiving $0.13. Therefore my potential loss is $1.87. Remember that the $1.87 number is for contracts worth 100 shares. Therefore the loss for one contract is $187. But I have sold 10 contracts to make it worth my while. Therefore my potential loss 5 percent of the time will be $1,870.

Let's do the math. 91 out of 100 times I will make $130. 130 × 91 = $11,830. Five out of 100 times I will lose the entire amount. 1,870 × 5 = $9,350. What about that missing 4 percent of the time where I may not lose all of it, but I will definitely lose some. Let's strike a happy medium and say that I will lose half of the $1,870 which is $935. 935 × 4 = $3,740. Now let's add the $3,740 to $9,350 that brings the loss to $13,090. Therefore your net *loss* statistically for 100 credit spreads at 10 contracts is $1,260.

We can do this over and over again for any combination of strike prices, expirations, and spread distances. The answer will be the same. From a purely statistical standpoint you will always lose money over the long run unless you can get better odds.


Can It Be Fixed?

There are all kinds of systems that you can read about that will try to mitigate the statistical risks that are involved in high-probability credit spreads. Obviously one of the real problems statistically is the large loss that will be incurred relative to the small premium that you will receive.

Obviously in the previous example a $0.13 premium with a $1.87 possible total loss is not a good ratio. This is less than a 7 percent return. What if I could find one with a 50 percent return?

I found a 31-day option with a $2.00 spread and a 0.28 Delta selling for $0.74. Let's see if it will work. The maximum profit is $74 per contract. The maximum loss is $1.26 for one contract or $126 per contract. This is a 58 percent ratio. The position will make 100 percent of the premium 72 percent of the time. Looking down at the Delta of the higher strike price we see that its Delta is 0.22. Therefore 22 percent of the time it will lose the entire $1.26. There is a missing 6 percent where it will fall with some loss but not necessarily all.

Let's do the math. 72 × $74 = $5,328 profit.

22 × $126 = $2,772 loss plus 6 × $63 (half of $1.26) = $378 loss for a total loss of $3,150. Statistically this will give you a *gain* for 100 spreads of $2,178.

If you can get your ratio high enough then high-probability credit spreads can make money.

Before you do any credit spreads you must do your homework just as we have done here. You have to see statistically if this particular credit spread is going to work. This of course is in the absence of any other information you may have relative to the stock involved.

Disaster Will Strike

The Delta is what we have been referring to in order to get our probabilities. This is based on what will occur 68 percent of the time or what is known as one standard deviation. This does not mean that this is the only thing that can happen. Or that these numbers can be relied upon as gospel.

There are of course times that two standard deviations or even three will occur. Disaster will strike. You just don't know when.

There are all kinds of ways to try to mitigate disaster. There are systems that require you to close out the position when you've lost a certain percentage. Or they have you close the position if the stock approaches the short strike by a certain amount. Of course all of the systems change your probabilities dramatically.

There are other systems that require you to roll down as the short strike is approached. Rolling down can be done with spreads just as it can be done with call options.

The problem is you don't always have that luxury. Just as with a stop loss limit order you may wake up one morning and find that the stock has declined past your short strike. And there's nothing you can do about it. Or, there might not be enough time to make any of these fixes successful.

These are risks that cannot properly be expressed in probabilities. Make sure that if you are going to sell credit spreads you never overextend yourself. Don't sell more contracts than you are prepared to lose. And know how much your total loss could be before you enter a contract. Remember that what can go wrong at some time it will.

## The Iron Condor

### The Basic Theory

The Iron Condor is made up of two credit spreads, an Out of the Money credit call spread and an Out of the Money credit put spread. The reason it is called a Condor is that the two spreads act as wings. In a strategy that has the term iron, it is made up of both puts and calls.

Remember that there is no such thing as a totally neutral strategy, in that you make money regardless of what the market does. Every strategy has a bias. That bias can be that either the market will go up, the market will go down, or the market will stay flat. In this case the bias is that the stock chosen will stay flat or within a range. If the stock reaches either the short call strike or the short put strike you will lose money.

### How Much Does It Cost?

What you're dealing with here are two credit spreads. Therefore there is no actual cost. You are receiving money into your account from both spreads. But your buying power is reduced. Assuming that the distance between the strikes for both the calls and the puts is the same, then your buying power is not charged for both of them. It is assumed that if you lose money, you can only lose the money in one direction. At expiration the stock cannot be at both the short call strike price and the short put strike price at the same time. Therefore the amount of margin and reduction of buying power that you are charged is simply the distance between the strikes minus the premium that you received from both of the credit spreads.

Let's assume that you sold an Iron Condor for a total of $2.80. The distance between the strikes is $5.00. Therefore the most that you can lose will be $5.00 minus the $2.80 premium you received for both of the spreads. You total risk is $2.20. Therefore your reduction in buying power will be $220 per Iron Condor contract sold.

### What Is the Risk?

This is the way an Iron Condor is constructed. Let's assume that the stock is selling for $50 per share. You sell a 55/60 call and at the same time you sell a 45/40 put. You receive a $3.00 total credit for both of them. Your risk for the entire Iron Condor is $2.00. This is the $5.00 distance of the spread minus the $3.00 credit.

Look at the risk graph in Figure 3.6. Your loss occurs at either of the short strike prices on both the upside and the downside. Your profit is maxed out for the amount of credit received. Notice that the risk graph for an Iron Condor is the same as the risk graph for the two credit spreads attached together at the top.

Can It Be Fixed?

The Iron Condor has all the risks in the caveats expressed in high-probability credit spreads. When evaluating whether or not the Iron Condor can make money, you should evaluate each spread independently using the same criteria that you did with high-probability credit spreads. This means that each credit spread must have enough premium independently to overcome the percentage odds.

If the above is taken into consideration then you can make money with Iron Condors. And in the long run you will make money. Remember that the Delta is talking about the percentages within one standard deviation. This means that the percentages will be correct 68 percent of the time. But stocks can move more than one standard deviation, and rapidly. When this happens a loss can occur without notice.

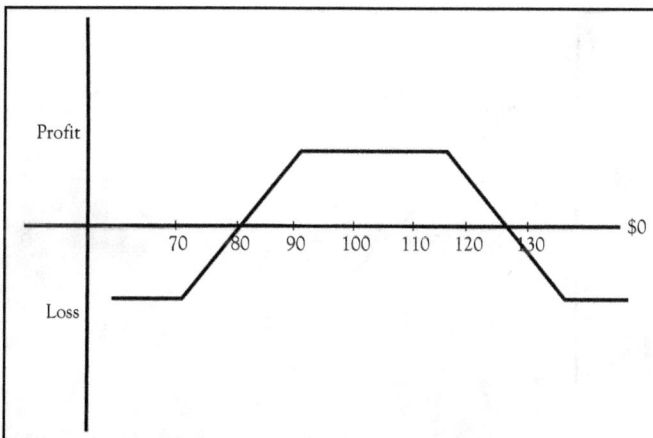

**Figure 3.6  Iron Condor**

If the stock rises or declines in an orderly fashion there are things that can be done to mitigate the loss just as with the high-probability credit spreads.

Let's assume that the stock declines to the put strike price. The call has now made money because the stock price is far away from the short call strike. But the put portion is starting to lose money. Nothing needs to be done with the call spread. And the put spread may be rolled down. If this does not solve the problem the call spread may be rolled up. In essence what you're doing is rolling the entire Iron Condor. Another alternative is to leave the initial call spread and simply establish a new one. Be aware that this will require more margin because you now have three credit spreads.

## The Straddle and Strangle

A straddle and a strangle are very similar to each other in that they both involve the simultaneous purchase of a call and a put. Let's look first at the straddle.

This is used when you think that a stock is due for a dramatic move one way or the other, but you just don't know which. Let's assume that in a few days earnings are coming out on your favorite stock. You don't know whether those earnings are going to be good or bad, but you do feel that one way or the other the stock is going to move. That is when you would buy a straddle.

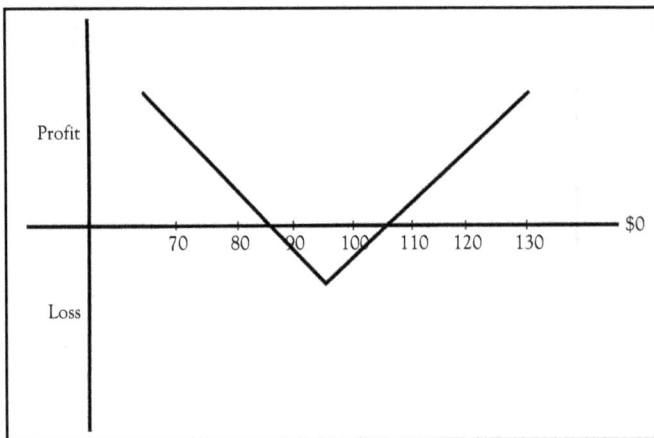

**Figure 3.7 Straddle**

The straddle involves purchasing a call and a put as close to At the Money as possible. Now it doesn't matter whether the stock moves up or down; either the call or the put will profit. The breakeven point is the sum total paid for both the call and the put added to or subtracted from the strike price.

The total risk is the amount paid for both the put and the call.

Look at Figure 3.7, the straddle. Notice it has a V formation. Each side of the V as it crosses the zero line is your breakeven. The straddle has a limited risk, limited only to the premium paid.

The problem with the straddle is that At the Money calls and puts are very expensive. And in fact around earnings time volatility increases dramatically and thus makes both the call and the put even more expensive than normal. If the stock does not immediately move on the earnings announcement the volatility will deflate like a punctured balloon. And your loss becomes almost immediate.

One way around the expensive straddle is the strangle. The strangle purchases a slightly Out of the Money call and a slightly Out of the Money put. This is substantially less expensive than purchasing the straddle. Since you are purchasing both the put and the call Out of the Money the stock must move further than with the straddle in order to make money on the strategy.

Notice in Figure 3.8 that instead of a V formation there is a flattening at the bottom which is the distance of the Out of the Money strikes.

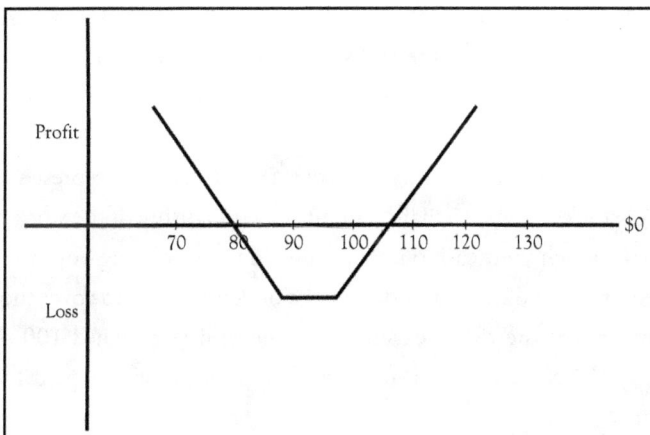

**Figure 3.8 Strangle**

# Synthetics

One of the many problems of buying long stock, selling stock short, or creating a covered call position or collar is that it is very expensive. This makes it very difficult for small accounts to purchase many shares of stock and participate significantly in small stock moves.

This is why simply buying long calls or long puts is so popular. But we have already seen how the odds of making money using the strategy are very bad.

That is where synthetics come in. A synthetic stock is a combination of options that have the exact or nearly exact risk graph as the stock, but are unbelievably less expensive. Synthetics do have one caveat. They carry no dividend. Unlike a stock which may pay a dividend, the synthetics are not stocks. They are simply a combination of options that together have the same performance characteristics of stocks.

### Synthetic Long or Short Stock

Let's assume that you wanted to purchase a stock selling for about $100. Let's also assume that your entire investing account was only $3,000. This means you could only afford 30 shares.

Instead of simply purchasing the stock you create a synthetic long position. Stock can be emulated by purchasing one At the Money call and simultaneously selling one put at the same strike.

I'm looking at a three-month call on a $100 stock. If you purchase the 100 strike call and sell the 100 strike put your total cash outlay is only $45. The Delta on this position is 0.9916. Remember that a pure stock position has a Delta of 1.00. What this means is for every $1.00 move in the stock the option position will move $99.16 (since it represents 100 shares of stock). This is virtually a one-to-one mirroring of the stock itself.

Even though your cash outlay is only $45 your buying power will be reduced by about $2,600 in order for the brokerage firm to cover the risk. Remember that the risk is exactly the same as if you owned 100 shares of stock. Therefore your risk far exceeds the $45 that you paid for the position.

The synthetic short stock is the exact opposite of the synthetic long stock. A synthetic long stock is buying the call At the Money strike and selling the corresponding put. To emulate short stock buy the put At the Money strike price and sell the corresponding call.

Besides the lesser amount of cash outlay there are other significant reasons why you would want to use a synthetic short stock instead of the real thing. For stocks with a significant following there is generally no problem in shorting them unless the short position is extremely high. But for lesser followed stocks you may not actually be able to short them because it does require a physical borrowing by your broker of stock from another account. The synthetic short stock presents none of these problems. Also if you are short the stock when it goes ex-dividend, then you owe the dividend.

Do remember that your risk incurred is exactly the same as if you held a short stock position. Theoretically your risk is unlimited if the stock goes up.

### Synthetic Covered Call

The covered call strategy is equally expensive because it requires the purchasing of the stock itself. Remember as a strategy you have a limited gain and an unlimited potential for loss.

You can create a synthetic position of the covered call strategy. Simply sell an At the Money put naked. Your profit potential is limited by the premium received from the selling of the put. Your potential loss because you are naked the put is unlimited or at least limited to what it would cost to purchase the stock at the strike price if the stock went to zero.

If the thought of selling a put naked At the Money makes you nervous then realize that using a covered call as a strategy should make you equally nervous since they have exactly the same risk. The only reason to sell a covered call is if you already own the stock and are planning on keeping it, but in the meantime you would like a little extra income. But be aware that if the stock goes up past the strike that you sold, you will have to sell your stock at that strike price.

# Hedge

What we are referring to here is a financial hedge. The definition of a financial hedge is the purchase or sale of one or more financial instruments in order to mitigate the risk and possible loss in another financial instrument.

The financial instruments do not necessarily have to be directly related. For example let's say that you own a portfolio of stocks that have run up considerably. You are afraid that the overall market is in for a correction, and if so, your portfolio may suffer a decline. In order to protect against this you purchase a treasury bond ETF. The theory is that as the overall market goes up, treasury bonds decline and vice versa. Therefore if there is a correction in the overall market the loss to your stocks will be mitigated by the appreciation of the treasury bond ETF.

### Characteristics of a Hedge

A good hedge is going to have several characteristics. Just because a hedge does not have all of these characteristics does not keep it from being a hedge. But you would like for it to have as many of these characteristics as possible.

1. The hedge must be easy to put on and take off as needed.
2. The hedge must limit your loss to an absolute known amount.
3. The hedge ideally should not put a *significant* cap on potential profit.
4. The hedge should be inexpensive.

### What Is and Is Not a Hedge?

Just because something may limit your loss does not necessarily make it a hedge. Let's use a roulette wheel as an example. Let's assume you want to put $2.00 on red which pays two to one. This means if red wins you get your initial $2.00 back plus $2.00 for a total of $4.00 and a $2.00 profit. If you lose and it comes up black or 0 or 00 then you lose your entire $2.00.

But you don't want to lose $2.00. The most that you want to lose is $1.00. So in addition to the $2.00 bet on red you place a $1.00 bet on black. Therefore if it comes up red you make $2.00 on red and lose $1.00 on black for a net gain of $1.00. If it comes up black then you lose $2.00 on red and make $1.00 on black for a loss of $1.00.

This is not a hedge. Even though you have technically limited your loss to $1.00 you could've done exactly the same thing by only betting $1.00 on red in the first place. Even though it is not technically a hedge it may serve a useful purpose. The table may have a $2.00 minimum. You might not be able to bet only $1.00 on red. In this way you have circumvented that restriction.

Another false hedge is the covered call. Even though your risk is somewhat diminished by the call premium received, it does not put any kind of limit on the downside risk. It is still total. Even the risk graph simply considers the call premium a simple reduction in the cost of the stock. In essence you have only put less money on red.

The hedge is designed to lose money. In fact if the hedge is making money it is doing its job of protecting you, but your main asset may be losing money. The purpose of the hedge is not to eliminate all risk. The purpose of a hedge is to mitigate that risk and at the same time permit the main asset to make money.

One of the simplest forms of hedges available to protect stocks is the put. As previously mentioned this is used as an insurance policy. Just as with an insurance policy, the hedge permits you to spend a little money to protect the underlying asset, and at the same time, it permits the underlying asset to continue to appreciate. If disaster does strike the put permits you to cap your loss at a predetermined amount. At the same time there is no limit on the potential gain.

If you own a stock that is selling for $50 per share and you want to protect it from a large loss you might purchase a 45 strike put for whatever period of time you feel the protection is warranted. This means if the stock declines beyond $45 per share your loss is capped at $5.00 per share plus the price of the put. This is because no matter how low the stock goes you can force the seller of the put to purchase your stock for $45 per share.

### Using Puts and Calls to Hedge

You can also protect your long position using not only puts but also calls. The main problem with using a put in order to protect a long position is that the puts are too expensive. If you annualize the cost of a put in order to protect your long position you will find that you may be spending 12 percent to 20 percent of the value of the long position that may only appreciate 8 percent.

This may be useful in the short run as a hedge that might be put on around an earnings announcement that may be volatile and then taken off after the announcement has been made.

One method that has been used in order to reduce the cost of a protective put is to simultaneously sell an Out of the Money call at the same expiration.

This is technically known as a collar. But what it really amounts to is a covered call with a protective put. We discussed this earlier.

Remember when we discussed the collar it was pointed out that it could be created with less cost and effort as a debit call spread. Therefore collars should not be used as a strategy. Use the debit call spread instead. The collar should only be used if you already own the stock and want to protect your position for a short period of time.

### One Hedge That We Will Use

We will be using the vertical call spread. This is a debit call spread. The vertical call spread is constructed by buying one At the Money call and selling one higher strike Out of the Money call. As the market goes up the At the Money call which we bought will increase in value faster than the higher strike call that we sold will lose money. This is because the At the Money call will always have a higher Delta than the further Out of the Money call which we sold.

We of course are putting a limit on the amount of money that we can make because a vertical spread not only has a limited risk on the downside, but also has a limited risk on the upside. This should not affect us because as the market goes up The Non-Timing Trading System will require us to close the position and take our profit long before we reach the upside limit.

Like the $2 limit on the roulette table, using a vertical call spread also has the advantage of giving us control over the cost of a single unit. We of course could also have a limited downside risk by simply buying a single At the Money call. The problem here is that since we are going to be using the SPY as our investment vehicle, the cost of a single At the Money call on the SPY may be more than we want to put at risk for a single unit. That excessive cost is like the roulette table minimum. We can't afford it. If our total investment capital is $5,000 we generally want a single unit to be around 10 percent or $500. A 90-day At the Money call on the SPY is generally substantially more than $500 even when volatility is low. So the vertical call spread has the advantage of reducing that cost.

## Expected Move

The expected move is a very powerful tool if used correctly. Its main purpose is to tell you what would be a normal move for a given stock over a given period of time. I think you would agree that it would be very helpful if you had some idea as to how far your stock could move over the next week, month, or any period that you choose. That is what the expected move does.

Before we can have a discussion on expected move, we have to understand the concept of volatility. Volatility in a stock or an option is synonymous with what the marketplace considers to be the risk of that stock or option. Therefore the term volatility is simply another way of expressing risk.

There are two types of volatility: historical volatility and implied volatility. Historical volatility is simply the volatility of the financial instrument over the past year. Implied volatility on the other hand is the volatility of the financial instrument right now. Implied volatility is implied by the value of the options that are being bought and sold.

To get the implied volatility we have to look at the options market. Even if you're not trading options, the options market can tell you a lot about what the marketplace thinks about the risk of a given stock. When you compute an expected move of a stock what you are actually doing is creating a distance of what is known as a standard deviation. Without getting too technical into statistics let's see what a standard deviation is. For now don't worry about how it's computed.

Look at Figure 3.9. This is a graph of what is considered to be a normal distribution. Some call this a bell curve. Each of the numbers at the bottom represents one standard deviation plus or minus. What this represents is that for any given population of data, be it test scores or in our case stock prices, the percentage of times that it will occur within the groupings that you see on the graph. Let's assume that one standard deviation to the right is our upper limit of our expected move and one standard deviation to the left is our lower limit. What this graph is telling us is that 68 percent of the time the stock will fall between the lower limit and the upper limit. We can further divide this by saying that 34 percent of the time it will fall toward the upper limit and 34 percent of the time it will fall toward the lower limit.

But you have to be very careful here. It is not trying to make a prediction. The expected move has no directional bias. It is not saying that the stock will reach the upper limit 34 percent of the time. And it is not saying that the stock will reach the lower limit 34 percent of the time. All it is saying is that if the stock does reach the lower limit or if the stock does reach the upper limit it would not be an unusual occurrence. It would not be out of the ordinary. In other words the expected move is not making a prediction as to whether the stock will go up or down nor how far.

But let's look now at that area outside of one standard deviation. That's actually the important area that will help us to make money. Let's start by assuming that the stock actually reached the upper limit. What is

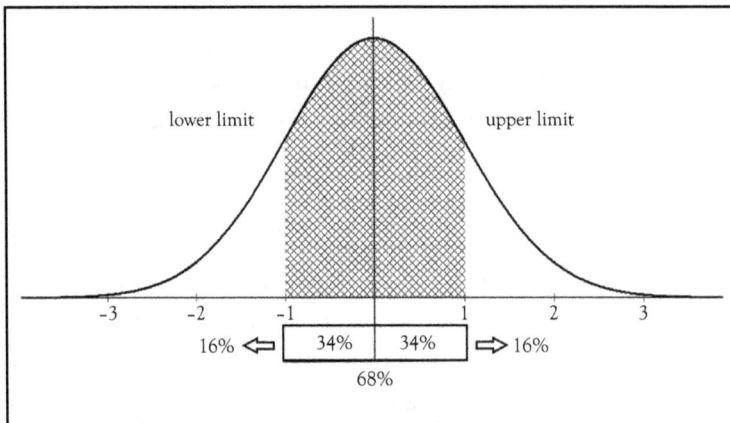

*Figure 3.9 Expected move*

the probability that it will continue to go higher? Or let's assume that the stock actually reached the lower limit. What is the probability that it will continue to go lower? Well, if 68 percent of the time it will fall between our upper and lower limits, meaning one standard deviation, then 32 percent of the time it will go beyond our upper or lower limit. This means that if our stock reaches the upper limit there is only a 16 percent probability that it will continue to go higher. And if our stock falls to our lower limit then there is only a 16 percent probability that it will continue to go lower.

The Non-Timing Trading System uses the expected move in order to calculate the target price where positions will be sold and profits taken, and to calculate the price at which additional accumulation will occur. But remember these are not buy and sell signals. The expected moves are simply telling The Non-Timing Trading System that once these limits are reached there is a much lower probability that they will continue higher or lower. This doesn't mean that they won't. Let's face it, 68 percent is a pretty good probability, but there is still a 16 percent chance that the price of the stock will continue past the upper or lower limit. The Non-Timing Trading System has the controls built in to its mathematical model to keep you from trying to catch a falling knife as a stock declines.

For our example let's start with a theoretical stock trading at $100. We see from our options chain for that stock that the implied volatility for the 16-day option expiration is 20 percent. The formula to find the expected move is rather simple. The formula is: *price of stock * implied volatility * $\sqrt{\text{the number of days}}$ / $\sqrt{365}$*. As you can see the stock price is multiplied times the implied volatility times the square root of the number of days for which you want the expected move then it is divided by 19.10. Why 19.10? Because that is the square root of 365, meaning the number of days in a year.

Let's plug in our numbers and see what we get.

$$100 \times .20 \times 4 \div 19.10 = 4.19$$

| Stock price | IV | $\sqrt{16 \text{ days}}$ | $\sqrt{365}$ | |
|---|---|---|---|---|

So now that we have this number for the expected move what do we do with it? Well, we're going to add 4.19 to our stock price of 100 and we're going to subtract 4.19 from 100. So therefore our upper limit would be 104.19 and our lower limit would be 95.81.

Notice that the expected move of $4.19 has no directional bias. It does not try to tell you that the stock will go up $4.19 or will go down $4.19. It is simply a mathematical computation based upon the implied volatility. This is the range that the stock is expected to trade for the next 16 days.

The implied volatility is created from the price of the option at any given point in time. And the price of the option is determined by the supply and demand of millions of dollars being traded.

Even though it is easy enough to put the formula in a spreadsheet, let's look now at how you can quickly find the expected move without having to go through all the math. If you have Think or Swim, open up any option chain. On the right-hand side of the option chain you will see the implied volatility. In parentheses next to the implied volatility is the ± expected move. Think or Swim's calculation of the expected move is about 80 percent of the true formula. If you are not using Think or Swim, multiply the formula by 0.80 to get the expected move we are using.

But what is the expected move really telling us? Think of the 68 percent that we talked about as being *normal, most of the time, nothing out of the ordinary*. Therefore what we are saying is that it is not unusual for the stock to move up or down during this period of time for the amount of the expected move. *It is not a prediction.*

How are we going to use the expected move? We're going to look at a 30-day period of time. Let's assume that the expected move for the SPY is $7.00. Wouldn't it stand to reason that if the SPY goes up by $7.00 it would not be statistically in our favor to hold out for more since there is only a 16 percent chance that it will exceed the $7.00.

On the other hand if the SPY drops by $7.00 there is only a 16 percent chance that it will drop any more. Therefore our upper and lower limits will be based on a 30-day expected move.

Why are we going to be using the 30-day expected move instead of some other period of time? We would hope that within those 30 days the price of the SPY would move to the upper limit of the expected move. That is where we will make our money.

Normally we will hold our position for a maximum of approximately 60 days. That is to say we will close out our position totally 30 days prior to expiration. If the expected move in either direction has not reached the 30-day expected move in either direction within 60 days, it would by then be safe to say that the determination of risk by the marketplace (marketplace sentiment of risk) may have changed. At that point we will create another upper and lower limit for the expected move based on the then current price of the SPY.

So when you are looking for the 30-day expected move you want to choose the one that is the absolute closest to 30 days. If you are given a choice, for example, between 28 days and 31 days of course you will choose 31 days. If you are given a choice between 29 days and 31 days then choose 29 days.

# CHAPTER 4

# Basic System

## The System Is Scaled according to the Capital Available

This basic system is designed with the small investor in mind. All examples that we use assume an account with a capital allocation of $5,000.

The amount of capital that you have will determine the width of the vertical call spread. With $5,000 or more available you will use a 10-point spread. With a 10-point vertical call spread on the SPY we will be putting at risk about $500 to $600 per unit. The basic unit will be described later in detail. If you have less than $5,000 use the following for the amount of capital that you have available. As your capital grows increase the point spread accordingly.

| Capital Available | Spread |
|:-----------------:|:--------:|
| $5,000 | 10 points |
| $4,500 | 9 points |
| $4,000 | 8 points |
| $3,500 | 7 points |
| $3,000 | 6 points |
| $2,500 | 5 points |
| $2,000 | 4 points |
| $1,500 | 3 points |
| $1,000 | 2 points |
| $500 | 1 point |

Obviously with less capital to invest you won't make as much money of course, but it will still meet the goals of the system, to make at least an average yearly return of 20 percent to 30 percent or more and to beat the Standard & Poor's 500.

If you have more than $5,000 available The Non-Timing Trading System can be scaled up in $2,500 increments. The system normally calls for an initial purchase of two units. Each time you cover (add units), you will add one unit. If you have more than $5,000 then use the following chart to determine the quantity of the initial units and the cover units.

The Non-Timing Trading System may be scaled up to any capital allocation. Even in excess of $50,000, you will simply change the investment vehicle from the SPY to the SPX (the stock symbol for the actual S&P 500) which is 10 times the value of the SPY and begin again with two units and follow the chart increasing every $25,000.

With $5,000:
Initial position is two units.
Each cover position is one unit.

---

With $7,500:
Initial position is three units.
First cover position is two units.
Each additional cover position is one unit.

---

With $10,000:
Initial position is four units.
Each cover position is two units.

---

With $12,500:
Initial position is five units.
First cover position is three units.
Each additional cover position is two units.

---

With $15,000:
Initial position is six units.
Each cover position is three units.

---

With $17,500:
Initial position is seven units.
First cover position is four units.
Each additional cover position is three units.

---

With $20,000:
Initial position is eight units.
Each cover position is four units.

---

With $22,500:
Initial position is nine units.
First cover position is five units.
Each additional cover position is four units.

---

With $25,000:
Initial position is 10 units.
Each cover position is five units.

---

With $27,500:
Initial position is 11 units.
First cover position is six units.
Each additional cover position is five units.

---

With $30,000:
Initial position is 12 units.
Each cover position is six units.

---

With $32,500:
Initial position is 13 units.
First cover position is seven units.
Each additional cover position is six units.

---

With $35,000:
Initial position is 14 units.
Each cover position is seven units.

---

With $37,500:
Initial position is 15 units.

First cover position is eight units.
Each additional cover position is seven units.

---

With $40,000:
Initial position is 16 units.
Each cover position is eight units.

---

With $42,500:
Initial position is 17 units.
First cover position is nine units.
Each additional cover position is eight units.

---

With $45,000:
Initial position is 18 units.
Each cover position is nine units.

---

With $47,500:
Initial position is 19 units.
First cover position is 10 units.
Each additional cover position is nine units.

---

With $50,000: use the SPX instead of the SPY.
Initial position is two units.
Each cover position is one unit.

---

Remember that the SPY is 1/10 the value of the Standard & Poor's 500. Once you reach $50,000 you have now 10 times the initial value of $5,000. It is now much more efficient at this level to work with the options of the Standard & Poor's 500 directly. The Standard & Poor's 500 symbol is SPX.

Therefore when working with the SPX, remember that everything must be multiplied by a factor of 10. The options on the SPX have an increment of approximately $5.00 instead of $1.00. In some cases you will see that the increments change to $25. Sometimes you will have to make adjustments to get a close approximation to the SPY. For example, your ideal increment might be a spread from 2,845 to 2,945. (Using the SPY you would normally be using a 10-point spread, but since the SPX has a factor of 10 you should be using a 100-point spread). You might not be able to get a spread of exactly 100 points. You might need to adjust and go from 2,845 to 2,950 since a 2,945 might not be available.

Even though you may have more than $5,000 available it is not recommended that you begin at a higher level. As you are learning you might either paper trade or begin with the minimum of $500. In that way your mistakes will not be very costly, but you will still have money at risk.

With money at risk you can see how your emotions play and at the same time have the confidence to follow the rules knowing that you can't lose that much. This will make you more comfortable using the covers since they will not involve as much risk to your overall capital and as such, emotions will be kept at a minimum. When you have more at risk than your comfort level and confidence will allow, costly mistakes will happen or you will abandon the rules.

Once you have a thorough understanding of The Non-Timing Trading System and have grown your confidence, begin for real with no more than $5,000 even though you may have more capital available to you. Once you have grown your account to $7,500 you should have enough experience to raise it to your capital level.

## Assumptions

Every system has basic assumptions. There is no such thing as a totally neutral system or money machine that will make money no matter what happens. Therefore it is important to understand the assumptions of any system.

### Stock Market Will Move Higher

The stock market as a whole will move higher over time. This is an important basic assumption. It has proven true over the last 100 years even through the worst of times. The worst of times of course was the great depression of the 1930s beginning in 1929. But even with that no one can argue that the Dow Jones Industrial Average is higher today than it was at the low point in 1929. The stock market has moved higher given enough time.

Think of the stock market as an Atlantic hurricane. All hurricanes that originate in the Atlantic will eventually move north. That is because of the rotation of the earth. But that is not to say that an Atlantic hurricane can't move sideways or south. Of course they do. This is because other factors such as high or low pressure or wind may interfere with its natural progression. But eventually if the storm is still intact, it will move north. Even with the best technology that we have today we cannot tell you when the hurricane will move north or at what angle with any degree of certainty. The same is true with the stock market. We know that it will be higher, but we don't know when or how much it will move sideways or down or when it will begin moving up again.

At the same time you do not want to be in the stock market during a major correction or a bear market. But you do want to be able to get back in when that correction or bear market is over.

### You Have a Minimum of $500 to Invest

The Non-Timing Trading System is designed for the small investor. The small investor is defined here as someone who has a minimum of $500 to invest. If you do not have $500 available to you, you should not be using the system.

All examples used are starting with a total capital of $5,000. Regardless of how much capital you are beginning with, as the system begins each time you will only be using 20 percent to 30 percent of the available capital. You always need the additional 70 percent to 80 percent in reserve. Even though we will be out of the market during major corrections or even a bear market, there will always be pullbacks that we want to use those funds to take advantage of.

### You Will Always Be in the Market

Except for major corrections, we will always want to be in the market. Just as we never know when the next major correction is going to occur or when the next bear market will begin, we also never know when the next major bull trend will begin.

We are going to be very skittish when our system tells us to get out. But absent that we want to be in the market to take advantage of major rallies. Most of the time we are not aware that we are in a major bull market trend until it is well underway. Then it is too late if we are not already in the market.

### You Never Know When the Bear Will Strike

You never know when the next bear or major correction will strike. You never want to be in a position to ride one out. Imagine being in the market from October 2007 through March 2009. Imagine every day saying it can't go any lower. That period of time was not fun if you were long the market.

We have set up a system where we will get out of the market no matter what. When The Non-Timing Trading System tells you to get out it is very important that you get out. The system may be wrong. You may be selling at a loss and then miss out on an opportunity. If that is the case the system will get you back in. But it is much better to take that small loss and miss the opportunity than it is to take a ride through a major correction. Over time you will come out better. And you will not be dealing with an emotional roller coaster.

### Nothing Lasts Forever

Irrational exuberance was the term Alan Greenspan used on December 5, 1996, to describe the stock market. His timing was off in warning about the .com bubble and the crash that was to come. But irrational exuberance is what occurs at the end of a major rally and bull market. No one believes that it can ever end.

It always does. And you must be ready.

At the other extreme, contrary to the popular belief at the time, the world will not come to an end, and the sun will come out tomorrow. The only question is when is that tomorrow going to be. In the case of the Great Depression it could take years. In the case of the crash of 2007 to 2009 it was over on March 9, 2009.

Nothing lasts forever, not even a bear market.

### You Are Not Predicting the Market

No one can predict the stock market! You cannot consistently time the market no matter what the guru's advertising says. There are just too many variables. And in today's market even machines are taking over and moving the market in different directions.

Charts can help if they are really simple and are simply used as a warning to get out. There are no technical indicators that are going to tell you consistently when to go long or short. All technical indicators are lagging. This means they tell you what has happened, not what is going to happen. There is no such thing as a crystal ball.

The Non-Timing Trading System does not try to predict the market. It simply follows the market. It starts with the assumption that the market will go up, and it wants you in the market when that happens. You may be in the market when the market is flat and doing nothing as was the case in 2015. And as such you may not make as much money.

Just because The Non-Timing Trading System does not try to predict the market doesn't mean that it won't recognize danger signs. And when those danger signs occur you need to get out. When the danger signs are over and the market has stabilized it will get you back in.

This isn't trying to predict the market. Just because there is a danger sign and we get out, it is not predicting that the market will go down and that we should short the market. And just because the danger signs are over and the market stabilizes does not mean that we are predicting that the market will go up. We simply want to be in the market when it does go up.

# Definition of One Unit

The strategy that we will be using is the vertical call spread. A unit consists of one spread. That means we will be buying one At the Money call and selling one Out of the Money call in the same expiration month. This spread constitutes one unit. So if the system says buy two units, then you will be buying two vertical call spreads. If the system says that you are buying or selling one unit then you will buy or sell one vertical call spread.

# What Makes a Stock or the Market Move?

One of the things that you need to remember is that stocks are not simply numbers on a page. These are actual companies that engage in a business that attempts to make a profit. When a company earns a profit year after year, pays a dividend, and continues to grow, then the value of that company increases. Analysis of these factors and how they determine the price of a stock now and in the future is called fundamental analysis.

But this does not explain the fact as to why Amazon, arguably one of the most successful companies with a very high stock price, failed to earn a dime for years. Yet the price of the stock continued to grow to what it is today. Companies like Amazon and many others have the price of their stock affected more by what people believe the company will do in the future than the actual earnings. Conversely when a company disappoints that expectation it can have devastating effects on the stock itself.

Related to this expectation of a company is what is known as technical analysis. Technical analysis is based on the belief that everything you need to know about the cumulative expectations of investors is expressed in the stock's chart. As individuals and funds buy and sell a given stock it creates patterns on the chart that, with proper analysis, can indicate the feelings and expectations of the investors and the possible future direction of the stock. Sometimes this technical analysis can actually turn out to be a self-fulfilling prophecy where those individuals and computers who are actually following the technical analysis act in common with what they see and affect the movement of the stock.

The third and probably most important factor that affects the short-term movement of the stock is the catalyst. A catalyst is a piece of news that may or may not be related directly to the company that causes investors to either buy or sell. This can be anything from a surprise earnings report, forward guidance by the company that is unexpected, the surprise resignation or hiring of a key individual, major company announcements, and even news reports unrelated to the company itself that might have implications to the economy as a whole.

As you can imagine this makes an individual company stock very vulnerable to these factors. An individual investor can do all the homework necessary to establish a true fair value for a company while at the same time be blindsided on the downside or the upside by one of these other factors. There is no way that the average investor can anticipate with any degree of certainty major catalysts. This is what makes short-term investment in individual stocks risky.

If all of these factors can affect the movement of individual stocks, then what can move the market as a whole. When we speak of the market we're generally speaking of market indexes. The best known of these market indexes is the Dow Jones Industrial Average, commonly known as the Dow. The Dow is made up of a weighted average of 30 industrial stocks. One of the problems with the Dow itself is that because it is made up of so few stocks, if one of those stocks has a severe problem, which can occur from time to time, you can dramatically skew the Dow so that it is not truly reflecting the health and direction of the market.

The other major index that is widely used is the Standard & Poor's 500. This index is made up, as the name implies, of 500 individual stocks. As you can imagine it is difficult for an index this massive to be moved by the performance of a single individual stock or even a sector of stocks. That is why the Standard & Poor's 500 is considered by many to be the bellwether of how the market is moving.

Then what does move the market as a whole? The answer to that is quite simple: a catalyst. Unless you're dealing with news about a very important bellwether stock, most catalysts are generally related to the economy, world news, or politics. In the absence of these catalysts the market generally just rolls along, going up some days and down other days. Then all of a sudden a catalyst appears in the market and it takes a sharp downturn or upturn or it begins a major trend in either direction. The problem is that a catalyst by its very nature is impossible to predict.

Sometimes exuberance or fear can be the catalyst. Most times it's hard to pinpoint exactly where this exuberance or fear began. It simply grows with time and creates what is known as a trend either up or down. The problem with these trends is that they are very difficult to identify until they are well underway, and by then it is often too late to join the party. And many times for the average investor, when the trend is well identified and when the exuberance or fear has reached its peak, it is then that the small investor finally jumps in.

# Use the SPY

The system and all the examples we use are based on using the SPY. The SPY is an ETF (Exchange Traded Fund) that mirrors the S&P 500 at 10 percent of its value. In addition the SPY has options available. This is ideal for the small account. Since the SPY and the S&P 500 encompass a large number of stocks, it provides the necessary diversity.

Also the option chain of the SPY is generally traded in increments of $1.00. This provides the flexibility necessary to control risk. This is especially important if your available capital is less than $5,000.

The SPY also has enormous liquidity, that is, the number of contracts that are open and traded. This will determine the spread between the bid and ask price of the option. If you are using a security without good liquidity then the distance between the bid and ask price will be very large and you will probably be overpaying for the option. In addition it may be difficult to close the position. You may be at the mercy of the market maker.

One final advantage of the SPY is that it provides weekly options. This means that we can get closer to a 90-day and 30-day expiration month.

The Non-Timing Trading System may work with other ETFs as long as they have substantial liquidity, and you are confident that over time their market will go up.

I would be very leery about using The Non-Timing Trading System on individual stocks. The first basic assumption of the system is that over time the market will go up. That cannot be said with any certainty about any given stock. When you're dealing with the SPY or other ETFs, there are enough stocks involved so that the risk is spread. With an individual stock on the other hand you are subject to bad decisions within the company, external economic forces, competitive environment, governmental regulation, and all of the other things previously mentioned that can affect the price of the stock.

# CHAPTER 5

# The Process

We are choosing to use the vertical call spread as the vehicle for our system. It is by no means the only strategy that you can use. The Non-Timing Trading System is actually a process, not a strategy. It simply uses a strategy such as the vertical call spread as the investment vehicle. And the vertical call spread is simple to execute and works very well.

It is the *process* that makes this or any other strategy work. The strategy itself is secondary. As long as it is a long strategy, that is to say that you make money when the market goes up, you have limited and known risk, and you can control the cost of a unit relative to the amount of available capital that you have, it should work. The difference in any strategy will have to do with the amount of risk/reward. Both the process and the strategy work hand in hand.

## Steps in the Process

### Step 1: Determine the Correct Expiration Month

The first thing that you're going to want to do is choose the correct expiration period. When you first go into the Analyze or Trade tab in Think or Swim you will see a bunch of dates. This is the date on which the option expires. Slightly to the right in parentheses is a number. This is the number of days from today until that expiration.

The expiration period should be 90 days or more. You want to choose the first expiration period that is 90 days or more. For example, if the number of days is as follows: 87, 107, 120 then you will choose the 107.

### Step 2: Determine the Strike Price

You will begin the strategy by purchasing one At the Money call per unit. This will always be your starting point. The question is which strike price should you purchase since it will be rare that a strike will be At the Money to the penny.

When you first look at the list of options for the SPY it can be overwhelming. That list of options is known as the option chain. Each expiration period has its own option chain. When you first look at the option chain you may not see enough strike prices. Look toward the top center and you will see the word *Strikes* followed by a drop box with a number in it. Either change that number to 40 or click on ALL. Now you should have plenty of strikes in the option chain.

In Think or Swim the In the Money options are a slightly different shade than the Out of the Money options. You may need to scroll down until you see the color changing from In the Money to Out of the Money.

It is almost impossible to find a strike that is absolutely At the Money to the penny. Therefore you are looking for the closest call strike that is *below* the current price of the SPY. For example, if the SPY is selling for 357.40, you would first look at the 357 call strike. Look first at the call side. Check the ask price of the call. Then look over at the corresponding put side of the same strike. Look at the put's bid price. You are looking for a call where the bid price of its corresponding put is larger than the ask price of the call.

If the put bid is more than the call ask then that is the strike that you will use. If on the other hand, the call ask is more than the put bid look to the next higher strike price. Even if the next higher strike does not have the put bid higher than the call ask, choose that one anyway. Do not use any higher strike price than those two.

### Step 3: Initial Entry Is Two Units

Your initial entry is going to be two units. (Throughout this section we will be referring to the number of units for entry, covering, or closing. These number of units are based on a total capital of less than $7,500. If your total capital is $7,500 or more and you are scaling up, then your number of units will be adjusted accordingly.) (See Chapter 4—Basic System.) Since a unit involves more than one option strike they should be done as a unit. Selling and buying them separately is called "legging in" because each call strike is one "leg" of the vertical call spread.

In Think or Swim it is very easy to create a combination order of up to four legs for individual calls or puts. For example: if you want to purchase a vertical call spread then click on the ask price of the call, hold your control key down, then click on the bid price of the higher strike call. What you will see is a combination order for both buying one call and selling the other. The price column will reflect the current mark (the halfway point between the bid and ask of the combination). If you're using another system other than Think or Swim, it should have a similar mechanism for creating a single spread. There are other methods even in Think or Swim, but this is one of the most efficient ways.

Since our initial entry is going to be two units you want to change the number of contracts from one to two.

### Step 4: Determine the Expected Move for 30 Days

After the units have been created the next thing that we need to do is to determine what is the expected move for 30 days. In Think or Swim, open up the expiration month closest to 30 days. If you find two expiration months, one with 29 days and the other with 31, then choose the one with 29. Since those two expiration months are equal distance from 30 you will be choosing the lower of the two.

Look to the right of the date and you will see the volatility of that particular expiration month expressed as a percentage. To the right of the volatility percentage in parentheses is a ± and the expected move.

Assuming that the current price of the SPY is 357.40 and that the expected move is 11.397, round the expected move to two decimal places which would be 11.40. Add 11.40 to 357.40 and subtract 11.40 from 357.40.

What you now have is the following:

Upper 368.80
Lower 346.00

What this is saying is that the SPY has a 68 percent chance of trading between 368.80 on the upside or 346.00 on the downside within the next 30 days. Of course we don't know which will happen or if either will happen. You will need to write these two numbers down, both the upper and the lower limits of the expected move.

### Step 5: When to Close or Cover

Getting in is one thing, knowing when to get out is quite another. Therefore we have established a set of rules for when to get out of the position and what to do once you are out.

With the exception of the emergency *get out* rule, closing all positions will occur on only three situations: (1) when the SPY has reached the upper expected move or one of the two alternative methods for determining this, (2) when the SPY has reached the lower expected move *and* you are less than 46 days from expiration, (3) when you are within 30 days of expiration.

When to Close

*Situation (1): Price of Stock Moves to the Upper Limit*

The reason we have established an upper and lower limit for the expected 30-day move is to tell us when to close our position and reestablish it at the new price or when to add to our position.

The first signal when to close your position is when the price of the SPY has reached the upper limit of the expected move. The closing of the positions may be done any time during the trading session. At this point certain positions will be closed (either all positions or just the positions used to cover). This should result in a profit.

Generally speaking you should be out before the upper limit is actually reached. Bulls make money, bears make money, hogs get slaughtered. This is an old saying on Wall Street. Imagine the SPY reaching within a few cents of your upper expected move where you could have closed the position for a profit. But because it did not get there to the penny you waited. The SPY then retraced and resulted in a loss. How would that make you feel? Here are two alternate methods of determining when to close as the SPY approaches the upper limit.

*Alternate Method One for Closing Upper Limit*

A few cents one way or the other is not going to make that much of a difference. Use $0.75 as your guide. Once the SPY has reached within $0.75 of the upper limit of the expected move close your position.

*Alternate Method Two for Closing Upper Limit*

An easy method for determining when to close as the SPY approaches the upper limit is by how much profit you will make per unit that you are going to close. This method has the advantage that you can predetermine the price at which you will sell your position. You can put in a "good til cancel" order to sell. In this way you do not have to be glued to the computer. If the price reaches your predetermined sell price, it will execute.

Of course you can use any profit amount that you wish. One that seems to work well is a profit of about 20 percent to 25 percent of your at risk money. Let's assume that the two units cost you $1,000. Then you are looking for a profit between $200 and $250.

Aren't you giving up some profit? What happens if the market continues to advance? Not really, remember that you are going to get back into the market if you closed all your positions, and in any event you will establish new expected moves, and you will use a new expiration month that will have more days until expiration and thus reduce the immediate effect of Theta. If the market does not continue to advance and begins to go down then your lower expected move where you will cover will be higher than before. And remember you have already locked in a profit.

**The reverse is not true on the downside. Do not cover until 3:30 p.m. or later and the price of the SPY has reached a point *equal to or less than the expected move*. There is no discretion on the lower limit.**

*Closing Positions*

It is easy to close a vertical spread. Remember that when we began the position we bought the vertical spread. You know that you are the buyer because it was a debit spread, meaning that it cost you money. The way to close any position is simply to create an opposite order. Since we bought the vertical spread, we will now sell the vertical spread. In Think or Swim you can simply create the sell order from scratch. But there is an easier way. There are several ways to do this but the easiest is to go into the monitor tab and to locate your spread in the Position Statement section. Highlight both legs of the spread and right click on your mouse. One of the options is to create a closing order. With more complicated orders there may be several ways to close them. But with the vertical spread there is only one way which is to sell the lower strike price and buy the higher strike price. That is of course the one you will choose. The order will then be created for your review.

Other brokerage platforms will have similar shortcut methods for closing basic positions.

### Start Over Again with Step 1, New Expiration Month, and Expected Move

When you have closed all positions due to the SPY having reached the upper limit of the expected move or one of the alternative methods, then you are going to want to reestablish your positions at the higher level. You will use the same criteria as you did when you began, establishing the new position with two units.

Just as you did when you initiated your position, you will also look at the 30-day expiration month at that time and establish a new expected move. Add and subtract the new expected move to the current value of the SPY in order to create a new upper and lower expected move limit. The old upper and lower limits of the expected move are no longer valid and should not be used again.

Even though you may have closed your position earlier, even at the open, I generally do not initiate a new position until at least 10 a.m. Eastern Time or maybe 10:30 a.m. There's an old saying on Wall Street that the first hour of trading is called amateur hour. Many times after the first hour of trading the market will have retraced a little bit from a hot opening.

### When to Cover

Previously we discussed when to close our positions when the SPY has reached the upper limit of the expected move. Now you are going to see what to do if the opposite has occurred. The SPY has reached the lower limit of the expected move.

### Situation (2): Price of Stock Falls to Lower Limit

Maybe the word *cover* is not a good term. It implies that you are doubling down. Doubling down just because you have taken a loss is a terrible idea and one of the quickest ways to the poor house. On a sustained downward move you will eventually run out of capital.

At the same time all stocks have an inevitable pullback following a run-up. This is their way of consolidating before continuing their upward move. Most pullbacks are minor and do not go beyond the 30-day expected move, some are more severe. Unless they are the beginning of a major correction or even a bear market, they can be viewed as an opportunity to add to your position.

Because volatility is affected by the severity of any pullback, the next 30-day expected move after a pullback will be larger since the market has declined, and the lower limit has been reached. What this means is that once a lower limit of the expected move has been reached a new upper and lower limit expected move will be created. And since the SPY is moving downward, volatility will be increasing and thus creating a higher expected move for the next 30 days.

Use 3:30 p.m. or later Eastern Time (one half hour before the market closes) to determine if the lower expected move has been reached. If it is reached before 3:30 p.m. then it doesn't count. Once it is 3:30 p.m. or later all the SPY has to do is reach the lower expected move or lower one time. It does not have to stay there. Ideally you want to cover at that very point. This is rarely possible. Execute your order as soon as possible regardless of where the price of the SPY is. There is no alternative method for determining the lower limit expected move as there is with the upper limit.

### Add One Unit Without Closing If >45 Days Remain

Once the lower limit expected move has been reached you are going to add one unit to your position. You will use the same criteria that you used in order to establish the positions except that you will create a one unit position instead of two.

If more than 45 days remain in the current expiration month you will continue to use the same expiration month that you used when you established the original position.

### Close All Positions If <46 Days Remain and Add One Unit to New Position

If less than 46 days remain in the current expiration month then close all positions. You are going to reestablish those positions using a new expiration month using the 90-day criterion that you used before.

If the lower limit of the expected move has been reached and you closed your positions because there were less than 46 days remaining in the current expiration month, you will now reestablish new positions with a 90+ day expiration month plus adding one unit. If this is the first cover that you have done your new position should now have three units.

### Create New Expected Move

Any time that you cover or close any positions you will always re-create a new expected move using the closest 30-day expiration month. This will create a new upper limit and lower limit. All of the previous expected moves are no longer valid.

### If New Upper Expected Move Reached Reduce to Two Units

Let's review our situation at this point. You began by opening your position with two units. At this point there are at least 90 days until expiration. You established an upper and lower expected move limit. The SPY has now come down and reached your lower limit expected move. You see that there are 50 days remaining in the current expiration month so you will use that same expiration month and open one additional unit. If less than 46 days were remaining you would have first closed all positions, then opened new positions with at least 90 days until expiration with three units.

Once you have the three units you established a new 30-day expected move with both the upper and lower limits. Now let's see what will happen.

You now have a new upper and lower limit for the expected move and a position with three units. Let's say that the SPY has now rallied and has reached the new upper limit of the expected move. If more than 45 days are still remaining in the expiration month simply close one unit and take what will probably be a profit on that one unit. The one unit that you will close will be the last unit that you opened (the one you used to cover). You now have the original two units remaining. And when you closed that one unit, the money that was withheld by the brokerage is released and your buying power increased back to its original two unit position.

Assuming once the new upper limit has been reached and there are not at least 46 days remaining in the expiration month, you will close all positions. You will now begin again with two units.

> In any event any time any upper limit expected move has been reached and you have more than two units open, then enough units will be closed (generally the one unit you used to cover) in order to get you back to a two-unit position. If you have four units open then you will close two units. Once the unit(s) has been closed then a new expected move for the upper and lower limits will always be reestablished.

Another way to state this is that any time an upper limit is reached and any position is closed you will begin a new expected move with only two units.

### If New Lower Expected Move Reached Add One Unit Using 46-Day Rule

Let's assume you currently have a three-unit position open because you were forced to cover. The SPY continues to decline after that first cover. It has now reached your new lower limit expected move. You will now add another unit again using the 46-day rule, giving you four open units. This means that if there are more than 45 days remaining in the expiration month, you will use the same expiration month and add the one unit. On the other hand if there are less than 46 days remaining in the current expiration month, you will first close all positions then reestablish the four-unit position using a 90+ day expiration month with the one additional unit.

**Any time an additional unit is added or units closed remember to reestablish a new expected move.**

When the SPY moves up to the upper limit expected move then close the last unit(s) you used to cover. For example, let's say that because of a severe decline you now have four units (your initial two units plus one unit each for two covers). The SPY now rallies and you reach the upper limit of the expected move. Close two units (the third and fourth units you used to cover). Reestablish a new expected move. If it continues to go up and reaches the new expected move then close the last two remaining units. On the other hand if it goes down to the lower limit then add one unit. Continue this as necessary.

Generally it will be rare to cover more than twice since an emergency *get out* will probably have occurred. The rules of how you get out when the market shows danger signs will not let it decline too much before the signal to close all positions is given. And remember as the market declines, volatility increases and as such, the range of the new expected moves increases as well. And this minimizes how many covers will be required.

Expiration

The reason that we used a 90+ day expiration month for our initial positions is to avoid the evil hand of Theta. Time decay is not linear. The major part of time decay occurs once there are 30 days or less remaining until expiration. Even though we have a hedge in place, which is by definition short and thus benefiting from time decay (positive Theta), our major position is long. Even though Theta is not really a big problem for us, a negative Theta will eat into the profits, especially if we were to maintain our position all the way to expiration.

*Situation (3): Close All Positions 30 Days Prior to Expiration*

In order to protect as much profit as possible we're going to always exit all positions once we have reached 30 days remaining until expiration. You may or may not actually have a profit. Depending on the price of the SPY at the time you close all positions, you may be at breakeven or even a loss. Regardless, all positions need to be closed 30 days prior to expiration.

From time to time you may actually have a positive Theta at 30 days prior to expiration. This is true if the SPY is substantially above your breakeven point on the risk graph. In this rare case you will have a positive Theta which actually works in your favor. I would still recommend that your positions be closed and you take your profit. This way you are protecting yourself from a sudden decline with very few days remaining until expiration. And you have also locked in that profit.

*Reopen Positions in New Expiration Month and Add One Unit*

If you have closed all your positions because you have reached 30 days prior to expiration, reestablish new positions and add one unit. Be sure to use the strike prices for the current value of the SPY. Use a new 90+ day expiration and establish new expected moves.

**You need to limit to one the number of times that you add a unit because of expiration during a given cycle.**

A cycle ends when the upper limit is reached and only the initial two units remain. No matter how many times you reach the 30-day limit during a cycle never add more than one unit. Adding that one unit because you reached the 30-day limit is a one and done. Do not keep adding units just because you continue to reach the 30-day limit without having reached an upper expected move.

If you have three units established because you have previously reached a lower limit and have never added a unit because of expiration then you may add one more unit bringing your total to four. Under no circumstances add a unit because of expiration if you already have four units established regardless of the reason they were added.

Let's assume that your initial positions 90+ days until expiration were based on a SPY with a value of 357.40. Now that you are 30 days until expiration you are forced to close all positions. The SPY has not reached either expected move. The SPY is now at 355.20. The new positions will be established at the 355 level, not the 357 original level. And one unit will be added since you only have two units working and have never added a unit because of expiration during this cycle. Therefore a three-unit position will be established.

*Create New Expected Move*

Any time any positions are closed for any reason a new 30-day expected move will be created. All other expected moves are no longer valid. Therefore since we closed all positions because we had reached a 30-day expiration and are reopening those positions with the 90+ day expiration month at the current existing level, we create a new 30-day expected move.

Treat the additional unit as though it were a cover. This means if the SPY goes to the upper expected move then remove any units more than two with >45 days remaining or close all positions with <46 days remaining and reopen with two units. If the SPY then goes to the lower expected move then add one unit with >45 days remaining or close all positions with <46 days remaining and reopen the previous number of units plus one.

# CHAPTER 6

# The Bear

## The Bear Can Strike at Any Time

The bear market of 2007 to 2009 was a 17-month bear market that lasted from October 11, 2007, to March 9, 2009. On October 11, 2007, was it possible to really understand that you were in the beginning of a bear market? By March 9, 2009, the S&P 500 was going to lose more than 50 percent of its value. At what point during the bear market, might you have come to realize that things could still get worse?

On September 21, 2018, the first down day following an all-time high of the SPY, did you really understand that a major correction was about to take place? The SPY was going to lose almost 20 percent of its value and drop as low as 234 from its high of 292. As a result calendar year 2018 was a losing year for the S&P 500 (but not for us).

On February 19, 2020, did you predict that the SPY would lose more than 120 points in only one month because of the covid-19 pandemic? Volatility went from 14.38 to 85.37. That kind of fear is panic territory.

The problem is you never know that you are in a bear market or any major correction until it is too late.

## How to Protect Yourself from the Bear

The Non-Timing Trading System is a defensive system. It is not trying to time the market and tell you when to go short. It is designed to tell you to get out when danger signals are present in order to protect you from what might happen. It is better to be out of the market until things stabilize even if you lose some opportunity. It is not trying to predict the market. It simply says get out because the odds are not with you.

In 2007 The Non-Timing Trading System recognized that there was something wrong on November 14, 2007, when the SPY closed at

145.54. The previous highest close had been 156.48 on October 9, 2007. That is only 10.94 points from the top of the market. It doesn't get much better than that.

It kept you out of the market until March 25, 2009. It signaled then that things were OK to get back in when the SPY closed at 81.85. The lowest close on March 9, 2009, was 68.11. You would have reentered the market only 13.74 points from the absolute bottom of the market. But the point is it kept you out during that long slide down.

### Create Two Moving Averages on the Chart

The rules that we are going to give you that will get you out of the market when things are not looking good and get you back into the market when things have stabilized are relatively simple. They do not involve complicated technical indicators such as Stochastics, MACD, or some other set of indicators. We're simply going to use two moving averages.

The first thing that you need to do is to create two moving averages. The first one is a 200-day *simple* moving average on a daily chart. The second is a 50-day *exponential* moving average on a daily chart. Of course you're going to want to make them different colors so that you can tell the difference between them at a glance.

The reason for the two different types of moving average is in order to be as conservative as possible. Typically a simple moving average during an uptrend is higher (has a higher average cost) than an exponential moving average. We are going to be using the 200-day simple moving average as our first trigger. Therefore when price closes below that moving average we want the moving average to be higher so as to give us an earlier warning sign.

On the other hand we want to know when the 50-day exponential moving average is within 1 percent of the 200-day moving average. In an uptrend the 50-day moving average will be above the 200-day moving average. As it approaches within 1 percent of the 200-day moving average it will be moving down. We wanted it to move down as fast as possible in order to give us an earlier warning sign. You will see what is meant very shortly.

### *Two Reasons to Get Out*

There are two major conditions where you must close all positions and get out of the market. Each condition involves a 200-day moving average and/or a 50-day moving average.

1. There is a sudden and drastic drop in price below the 200-day moving average. Close immediately.
2. Price closes below the 200-day moving average and
   A. the 50-day moving average is <1 percent above the 200-day moving average. Close immediately.
   B. the 50-day moving average is ≥1 percent above the 200-day moving average. Use the five-day rule.

### Condition 1. Sudden Drastic Drop in Price Below the 200 MA

We will use a 5 percent drop in one trading day as our definition of what is a sudden and drastic drop in price. You are going to measure from the close of the first trading day to the low of the next trading day. Here is the math. Assume that the market closes at 252.75. Multiply 252.75 × 0.95 = 240.11. 240.11 is your key number. If the low of the next trading day is ≤240.11 wait until the end of the day and see if the price is below the 200-day moving average. If it is below the 200-day moving average you must pull the rip cord and close all positions. You do not want to close immediately at the low just because it reached the 5 percent level. There is a really good chance that the market will close higher than that low. Even if it doesn't then it shouldn't move too much lower.

A drop of this nature is generally caused by panic selling early in the trading session. It will have a tendency to recover somewhat. But this kind of panic selling as it crosses the 200-day moving average is not a good omen. It has a tendency to build. This will not happen often, but if it does, get out.

Remember all technical indicators are lagging. They are a reflection of what has already happened. Moving averages are no exception. But they can indicate when you are in a trend, either up or down. They are never going to find an absolute top or an absolute bottom by definition.

Condition 2. Price Closes Below the 200 MA

If the price closes below the 200-day moving average it is a trigger point. It does not mean that you should necessarily close all positions at that point. Has the price of the SPY closed below the 200-day moving average? This normally needs to be a substantial drop, not just a little dip below. Here's the way you should judge a substantial drop. Look at the body of the candlestick. If more than half of the body closes below the 200-day moving average consider that a substantial drop. You don't want to be forced out of the market because of a meaningless dip. If you are unsure you can always wait one more day.

Check If the 50 MA <1 Percent above the 200 MA

As long as the price of the SPY stays above the 200-day moving average there is nothing that needs to be done. You are in good shape even if the price is retracing. As the price begins to move dangerously close to the 200-day moving average you need to begin your preparation.

You need to always be aware of the distance of the 50-day moving average to the 200-day moving average. Make a note as to the percentage difference between the two.

Here is the math that you will use:

Here are sample numbers for the two moving averages. Assume that the 200-day moving average is 276.23, and the 50-day moving average is 286.97. Here is what you want to know. Is the 50-day moving average <1 percent above the 200-day moving average?

Take 276.23 (the 200-day moving average) and multiply it times 1.01. The answer is 278.99. If the 50-day moving average is 278.99 or higher then the 50-day moving average is *not* less than 1 percent higher than the 200-day moving average. In this case 286.97 is substantially higher than 278.99 therefore the 50-day moving average is substantially higher than 1 percent of the 200-day moving average.

Let's move on a few days. Now the 200-day moving average is 275.84 and the 50-day moving average is 278.37. Let's multiply 275.84 (the 200-day moving average) by 1.01 and the answer is 278.60. The 50-day moving average is below the 1 percent level since it is lower than 278.60.

Therefore the question that you are asking is:

Is the 50-day moving average <1 percent above the 200-day moving average? Yes or No?

### If the 50 MA <1 Percent Above the 200 MA, Close All Positions

If at 3:30 p.m. Eastern Time or later (one half hour before the close of the market) the price has closed below the 200-day moving average (trigger point) *and* the 50-day moving average is less than 1 percent above the 200-day moving average then close all positions immediately. If the 50-day moving average is less than 1 percent above the 200-day moving average, **it does not have to be a substantial close below.** Any close below the 200-day moving average with the 50-day MA <1 percent will require you to close all positions. This is because the 50-day moving average is also dropping and is close to a crossover. There are a lot of algorithms out there that once the crossover occurs, big money managers will be selling.

### If the 50 MA ≥1 Percent Above the 200 MA, Use the Five-Day Rule

If the price has closed substantially below the 200-day moving average and the 50-day moving average is ≥1 percent above the 200-day moving average then you will use the five-day rule to determine if and when you will close your positions.

The five-day rule:

1. Always use 3:30 p.m. Eastern Time (one half hour before the close of the market on the fifth day).
2. Count five trading days from the close below the 200-day moving average (not counting the day of the drop).
3. If on the fifth trading day the price is not above the 200-day moving average, close all positions.
4. If on the fifth trading day the price is above the 200-day moving average remain in your positions.
5. If during the five-day count the two averages are <1 percent of each other and the price closes below the 200-day moving average, close all positions.

### What Happens Next After a Forced Close?

Once you are forced out of the market by either a sudden drastic drop, the 1 percent rule, or the five-day rule, two situations may occur. First the system might have gotten you out prematurely and a correction did not take place. Second the system got you out correctly and a correction did take place.

### Reentering the Market

How you get back into the market will depend upon which of the above situations occurs. Let's begin with the possibility that the system might have gotten you out prematurely. Here is what you are looking for in order to get back in.

We are going to define a correction a little differently than the traditional definition. Find the last time price was above the 200-day moving average. Then find the *highest close*. This should be the *highest close* of the first substantial leg up that was still *above* the 200-day moving average. Multiply that *highest close* by 0.90. This will give you a 10 percent correction number. Next find the *lowest low* following that last highest close. If the *lowest low* is less than or equal to the 10 percent correction number then a correction has taken place. If the *lowest low* is greater than the 10 percent correction number then a correction has not taken place.

If a correction has *not* taken place then the system got you out prematurely. In that case your next trigger line to reenter the market will be the 200-day moving average. If a correction has taken place then the trigger line to reenter the market will be lower of the 50-day moving average or the 200-day moving average.

Therefore we are looking for the price to close substantially above the trigger line. We will use the criterion of substantially based on 50 percent of the body of the candlestick closing above the line just as we did in looking at the candlestick when it closed below the 200-day moving average. Remember here that when we use the close we are talking about **the closing price at the absolute end of the trading session, *not* 3:30 p.m.** If that has occurred we will use the following five-day rule.

Notice that on the fifth day of the five-day rule, in addition to the price being above the trigger line, it must also be above the higher of the opening price or the closing price of the day that it first closed above the trigger line. We are looking for the highest part of the body of the candlestick. We will consider this the trigger day that begins the five-day rule. What we are looking for on the fifth day at the close (3:30 p.m.) is for the price to be above the top of the body of the candle of the trigger day (the day it first closed above the trigger line). We do not want to reenter if the market is falling.

Five-day rule:

1. Count five trading days from the close above the trigger line (not counting the day of the close above—the trigger day).
2. If at 3:30 p.m. Eastern Time on the fifth trading day the price is greater than the highest part of the trigger day's candle body then reenter the market.
3. If by the *close* of the trading session the price is not greater than the highest part of the trigger day's candle body then do not enter the market.
4. You may use a rolling five days. When using a rolling five days, the next day (day 2) is the new trigger day.

What a rolling five days means is that after the five days if the price is not above the trigger line you can test with day 2. If day 2 is above the trigger line then use day 6 for your five-day rule. If day 2 is not above the trigger line then test for day 3 using day 7 as your five-day rule, and so on.

If the five-day rule fails and you do not reenter the market but there was a close above the 200-day moving average, then you must reestablish a new 10 percent correction criterion, meaning that a new correction must take place before the 50-day moving average can be the new trigger line for reentering the market.

What happens after you reenter the market and there is another pullback below the 200-day moving average (if that was your trigger line) or below the 50-day moving average (if that was your trigger line) before the upper limit is reached? Where is the 50-day moving average at this point?

After you have reentered the market you will use the lower of the 200-day moving average or the 50-day moving average as your close-out trigger line. That is to say the price must close below that trigger line in order to begin the five-day rule to again close all positions. If you are forced out a second time use whichever trigger line forced you out as your reentry trigger line.

## How Do You Reenter the Market?

How you reenter the market again will depend on the price that is in effect at the time that you are reentering. Remember that when you were forced out of the market there was a lower limit expected move in effect at that time. If when you are reentering the market, you are reentering at a price which is above that previous lower limit expected move then reenter with the same number of units that were in effect when you closed all positions.

On the other hand if when you are reentering the market you are reentering at a price which is below that previous lower limit expected move, then reenter with the same number of units plus one that were in effect when you closed all positions.

Here's an example. Let's say that you had three units open at the time you were forced to close all positions. The lower limit expected move at that time was 354.10. There was a correction and you are now reentering the market at 352.47. Since you are reentering the market at a price which is lower than the previous lower limit expected move when you closed the positions, you should reenter with four units (one more unit). This is like adding one unit to cover, only it has been delayed by the correction.

After you have reentered and established your positions, reestablish new upper and lower limit expected moves.

If, after you have reentered the market, the price drops below your trigger line again, use the five-day rule to determine whether you're going to get out or stay in and cover. What this means is that you should check to see on the fifth day whether the price is above or below the trigger line. If the price is below the trigger line on the fifth day then again get out. If the price is above the trigger line on the fifth day and it is still below your lower limit expected move then you may cover. If the price is above the trigger line on the fifth day and is not below your lower limit expected move then there is no need to cover.

Now let's talk about what will happen when the upper limit expected move is reached. This means that you reentered the market, and the market continued to go up and reached your upper limit expected move within $0.75 or your maximum profit. This is for the profit on your total position, not just any units that were used to cover. Remember you do not have to wait until 3:30 p.m. Eastern Time. Since it's an upper limit expected move it can occur at any time during the trading day.

When the upper limit expected move has been reached close all positions. Do not reenter again until the 50-day moving average is ≥1 percent above the 200-day moving average. **What this means is that after a correction and you reenter the market, it is a one and done.** When you close that one trade because the upper limit expected move has been reached, do not trade again until such time as the 50-day moving average is ≥1 percent above the 200-day moving average.

If after you reenter the market you are forced to close all positions because you are within 30 days of expiration and not because of reaching the upper limit expected move, then it is not a one and done. You may reestablish your positions and maintain them until the upper limit expected move has been reached.

You might be asking why we are using a five-day rule to reenter the market. Why don't we just wait for a price crossover on either the upside or the downside. The problem is the 200-day moving average and the 50-day moving average are triggers for a lot of money managers and institutions and a lot of computer algorithms. When there are crossovers they may not be real. Waiting five trading days will avoid a lot of whipsaws.

Why is it a one and done? After a correction many money managers and computer algorithms tend to jump in when a crossover of the 50-day moving average or the 200-day moving average occurs. This massive buying creates the impetus for an upward move. Once this upward move plays out there generally is a pullback. The move upward may not be real and long lasting. And there may be a series of whipsaws (ups and downs) until a true trend has been established. We will not know that the trend is well under way until the 50-day moving average is ≥1 percent above the 200-day moving average.

Once the 50-day moving average is ≥1 percent above the 200-day moving average you may trade again immediately. You do not have to wait on the five-day rule.

# CHAPTER 7

# Decision Tree Recap

There have been so many rules thrown at you that it is hard to keep them straight. It might be even harder to find where in the book they were discussed. Therefore the following is a recap of the process. At any point in time all you have to do is find where you are in the process and follow the decision tree to tell you what to do and when to do it. This is a recap and should not be a substitute for reading a fuller explanation of the process. If the recap is unclear go back and reread that section.

I. Establish position with expected moves.
1. Begin with two units 90 days until expiration.
2. Find expected move using 30 days until expiration.
3. Establish upper and lower limits by adding or subtracting expected move to entry point.
II. Upper or lower limit reached.
1. Upper limit reached.
   *a.* Close positions.
   *b.* Go to *I.*
2. Lower limit reached.
   *a.* >45 days remain until expiration?
      A. Yes.
         i. Establish one additional position.
         ii. Use existing expiration.
         iii. Establish new upper and lower limits.
      B. No.
         i. Close all positions.
         ii. Establish new positions plus one.
         iii. Establish new upper and lower limits.

    *b.* If additional units have been added and upper or lower limits reached.

        A.   Upper limit reached with >45 days until expiration.

            i.   Close all units above two.

           ii.   Establish new upper and lower limits.

          iii.   Leave existing two units until either upper or lower limit or 30 days until expiration.

          iv.   Go to *II*.

        B.   Upper limit reached with <46 days until expiration.

            i.   Close all positions.

           ii.   Begin again with two units. Go to *I*.

        C.   Lower limit reached: go to *II→2*

III. 30 days prior to expiration.

    1.   Close all positions.

    2.   Has additional position been created because of expiration?

        *a.* Yes.

           A.   Establish same number of positions 90 days until expiration.

           B.   Establish new upper and lower limits.

        *b.* No.

           A.   Establish new positions plus one.

           B.   Establish new upper and lower limits.

IV. Forced to close because of potential correction.

    1.   Market above 200-day moving average—*Do Not Close*.

    2.   Market below 200-day moving average.

        *a.* One day dramatic drop below the 200-day moving average.

           A.   Multiply the close of the day before the drop by 0.95; this will give you a potential 5 percent drop.

           B.   Find the low of the day of the drop.

           C.   If drop is ≥5 percent then close at end of day.

           D.   If drop is not ≥5 percent then go to *IV→2→b*.

        *b.* Substantial close below—1/2 candle body below 200-day moving average.

           A.   No.

              i.   50-day moving average <1 percent above 200-day moving average—close all.

ii. 50-day moving average ≥1 percent above 200-day moving average—do nothing.

B. Yes.

i. 50-day moving average <1 percent above 200-day moving average—close all.

ii. 50-day moving average ≥1 percent above 200-day moving average—use five-day rule.

(a) Always use 3:30 p.m. Eastern Time (one half hour before the close of the market).

(b) Count five trading days from the close below the 200-day moving average (not counting the day of the close).

(c) If on the fifth trading day the price is not above the 200-day moving average close all positions.

(d) If on the fifth trading day the price is above the 200-day moving average remain in your positions.

(e) If during the five-day count the two averages come within <1 percent of each other and the price is below the 200-day moving average, close all positions.

V. Reenter the market after a forced close.

1. Definition of a correction.

   *a.* Find the last time price was above the 200-day moving average. Then find the *highest close*. This should be the *highest close* of the first substantial leg up that was still *above* the 200-day moving average.

   *b.* Multiply that *highest close* by 0.90. This will give you a 10 percent correction number.

   *c.* Find the *lowest low* following that last highest close.

   *d.* If the *lowest low* is less than or equal to the 10 percent correction number then a correction has taken place.

   *e.* If the *lowest low* is greater than the 10 percent correction number then a correction has not taken place.

2. Find the trigger line.

    *a.* If a correction took place the trigger line will be the lower of the 50-day moving average or the 200-day moving average.

    *b.* If a correction did not take place the trigger line will be the 200-day moving average.

3. If there is a substantial crossover of price above the trigger line then use the five-day rule. The day of the crossover of price above the trigger line is the trigger day. Substantial means at least half of the candle body is above the trigger line.

    *a.* Count five trading days from the close above the trigger line (not counting the day of the close above—the trigger day).

    *b.* If at 3:30 p.m. Eastern Time on the fifth trading day the price is greater than the highest part of the trigger day's candle *body* then reenter the market.

    *c.* If at the close of the trading session the price is not greater than the highest part of the trigger day's candle *body* then do not enter the market.

    *d.* You may use a rolling five days.

4. After you reenter, it is a one and done when you reach the upper limit.

    *a.* Do not trade any more until the 50-day moving average is ≥1 percent above the 200-day moving average.

    *b.* Once the moving average closes ≥1 percent above the 200-day moving average you may trade immediately. You do not have to wait for a five-day rule.

5. What happens if the market goes down after you have reentered and before reaching the upper limit?

    *a.* The new close-out trigger line is the lower of the 50-day moving average or the 200-day moving average.

    *b.* Market above the new close-out trigger line—*Do Not Close.*

    *c.* Market below the new close-out trigger line.

        A. One day dramatic drop below the previous trigger line.

            i. Multiply the *close* of the day before the drop by 0.95; this will give you a potential 5 percent drop.

            ii. Find the *low* of the day of the drop.

      iii.   If drop is ≥5 percent then close at end of day.

      iv.   If drop is not ≥5 percent then continue to next step.

B.   Substantial close below—1/2 candle body below the new close-out trigger line?

      i.   No.

          (a)   50-day moving average <1 percent above 200-day moving average—close all.

          (b)   50-day moving average ≥1 percent above 200-day moving average—do nothing.

      ii.   Yes—use the five-day rule.

          (a)   Always use 3:30 p.m. Eastern Time (one half hour before the close of the market).

          (b)   Count five trading days from the drop below the new close-out trigger line (not counting the day of the drop).

          (c)   If on the fifth trading day the price is not above the new close-out trigger line, close all positions.

          (d)   If on the fifth trading day the price is above the new close-out trigger line, remain in your positions.

# CHAPTER 8

# Tutorial—The System in Action

You've been given a lot of information concerning The Non-Timing Trading System. Some of it may be a little confusing to you at this time. Nothing works better than a tutorial complete with commentary on what is going on in order to give you a better understanding of how The Non-Timing Trading System works.

The examples in this tutorial occurred between November 1, 2013, and October 18, 2018. This is a five-year period. During that period of time there were three major corrections and one false correction. The Non-Timing Trading System successfully got you out in plenty of time during the three major corrections and kept you in during the false correction. In the S&P 500, 2014 was a fairly decent year, 2015 was flat, 2016 was decent, 2017 was fantastic, and 2018 actually resulted in a loss for the calendar year for the S&P 500 even though for our fiscal year the S&P 500 had a profit.

For the calendar year 2018, the S&P 500 suffered a loss of 7.6 percent. Since we were forced to exit in October 2018, we actually had a 21.74 percent gain for the calendar year.

Therefore this is a good five-year cross section of the market.

In each of these years The Non-Timing Trading System did better than the S&P 500. The average yearly return over the five-year period was 34.06 percent whereas the average yearly return of the S&P 500 over the same time period was 12.16 percent.

The trades depicted in the following tutorial during this five-year period were never actually put on. Instead it was an end-of-day simulation using Think or Swim's "Thinkback" system. Since this is an end-of-day simulation we were able to use the $0.75 discretion for the upper limit or the fixed-dollar amount option.

The information listed for calendar years 2019 and 2020 beginning in April 2019 was from actual trades that were executed using the fixed-dollar gained method of exiting.

It is valuable not only to show that The Non-Timing Trading System does work over a long period of time, but is illustrative as to what should be done using the system in each one of the circumstances. For each trade there is substantial commentary on why the trade was made and at what price.

It would be valuable if you would follow along with each of the trades while looking at a chart of the SPY complete with the two moving averages. In this way you can visually see what was happening with each trade.

In order to be as conservative as possible as to the capital available at each point, the $5,000 starting capital is never increased if it is in excess of $5,000. On the other hand during losing periods the $5,000 available capital is decreased with each closing trade if it is below $5,000. The capital does not return to $5,000 until such time that it has gained enough to exceed the initial $5,000. In this way you can see at any point in time what the true draw down is.

The percentage gain each year is based on $5,000 invested. In reality the entire $5,000 is never actually invested and put at risk. Most of the time it is only $1,000 to $1,800 working at any one time. Even though the percentage gain each year is impressive based on $5,000, the reality is that it is substantially much higher based on the average amount of capital actually at work at any one time.

Please do not just gloss over this tutorial. Look at each trade as though you were actually trading. Along with the commentary you will get the feel of how The Non-Timing Trading System works and many of your questions will be answered.

Ten-Point Long Call Spread

*November 1, 2013*

| Status | Open/ Buy | Units | 2 | P/L | | Upper | 180.94 |
|--------|-----------|-------|---|-----|--|-------|--------|
| Date | 11/01/13 | Strike | 176/186 | Equity | 5,000.00 | Cost | 750.00 |
| SPY | 176.21 | Days | 112 | +/– | 4.73 | Initial BP | 5,000.00 |
| Exp | Feb 21 | Price | 375.00 | Lower | 171.48 | End BP | 4,250.00 |

Let's begin by taking a look at how the data is portrayed in each one of these examples.

*Status:* There are four possible conditions. Open/Buy: Buy the number of units to open. Close/Buy: All open units will be sold and closed and new units will be bought and opened. Close Units: You will sell and close the number of units specified. No additional units will be bought and opened. This will always be the last units purchased. Close All: All open units will be sold and closed and no new units will be bought and opened.

*Date:* Date of the trade.

*SPY:* This is as close as we can get to the price of the SPY at any given time during the trade. In live trading the actual execution would be occurring many times between 3:30 and 4:00 p.m. or earlier in the trading day. Therefore the price of the SPY would be constantly changing.

*Exp:* Expiration month that was used.

*Units:* The number of units purchased.

*Strike:* The strike price of the options in the spread. The order in which they are presented is as follows:

The first number represents the strike of the long call purchased and the second number is the strike of the short call sold.

*Days:* Number of days remaining until expiration.

*Price:* Total cost of one unit for the long call spread purchased. *Cost* is where you will find the amount of money actually spent to purchase the total units in the spread.

*P/L:* The profit/loss any time a position is closed.

*Equity:* The actual equity position at any point in time. This will only change when a position is closed and the profit/loss is calculated.

*+/–:* The expected move for 30 days.

*Lower:* The lower limit for the expected move. This number is subtracted from the value of the SPY.

*Upper:* The upper limit for the expected move. This number is added to the value of the SPY.

*Cost:* The total cost for the transaction. This is the price for one unit listed in *Price* times the number of units listed in *Units*.

*Initial BP:* The buying power prior to the transaction.

*Ending BP:* The resulting buying power remaining after the transaction. Any time all positions are closed, buying power will revert to no more than $5,000.00 even though we may have grown our equity. Any loss will be subtracted from the *Initial BP*. Since the cost of our last trade was $750.00 our buying power has been reduced to $4,250.00.

*November 27, 2013*

| Status | Close/ Buy | Units | 2 | P/L | 330.00 | Upper | 185.87 |
|--------|-----------|-------|-----|--------|----------|------------|----------|
| Date | 11/27/13 | Strike | 181/191 | Equity | 5,330.00 | Cost | 724.00 |
| SPY | 181.12 | Days | 114 | +/– | 4.75 | Initial BP | 5,000.00 |
| Exp | Mar 21 | Price | 362.00 | Lower | 176.37 | End BP | 4,276.00 |

The upper limit expected move is reached and all positions are closed. New positions at the current level are established using two units.

*February 3, 2014*

| Status | Open/ Buy | Units | 1 | P/L | | Upper | 181.00 |
|--------|-----------|-------|-----|--------|----------|------------|----------|
| Date | 02/03/14 | Strike | 174/184 | Equity | 5,330.00 | Cost | 363.00 |
| SPY | 174.17 | Days | 46 | +/– | 6.83 | Initial BP | 4,276.00 |
| Exp | Mar 21 | Price | 363.00 | Lower | 167.34 | End BP | 3,913.00 |

The lower limit expected move has been reached and one unit is being added. This additional unit costs $363 and its buying power is reduced to $3,913.00. Since there are more than 45 days remaining we will use the same expiration as our initial two units. We now have three units active. New expected moves are created.

*February 11, 2014*

| Status | Close/ Buy | Units | 2 | P/L | 250.00 | Upper | 187.21 |
|--------|-----------|-------|-----|--------|----------|------------|----------|
| Date | 02/11/14 | Strike | 182/192 | Equity | 5,580.00 | Cost | 740.00 |
| SPY | 181.98 | Days | 94 | +/– | 5.23 | Initial BP | 5,000.00 |
| Exp | May 16 | Price | 370.00 | Lower | 176.75 | End BP | 4,260.00 |

The market proceeded to rally and the upper limit has been reached. All positions are closed. We made a $250 profit on our three units. The cycle begins again. Two new units are established.

If there had been more than 45 days remaining until expiration we would have just closed the one unit which we used to cover and left the other two intact. But there are only 37 days remaining until expiration. Therefore all positions are closed and two new units are established. Any time a cover is closed we always revert back to two units.

*March 4, 2014*

| Status | Close/ Buy | Units | 2 | P/L | 446.00 | Upper | 193.12 |
|--------|-----------|-------|---|-----|--------|-------|--------|
| Date | 03/04/14 | Strike | 187/197 | Equity | 6,026.00 | Cost | 834.00 |
| SPY | 187.58 | Days | 108 | +/– | 5.54 | Initial BP | 5,000.00 |
| Exp | Jun 20 | Price | 417.00 | Lower | 182.04 | End BP | 4,166.00 |

The upper limit expected move has been reached. All positions are closed and the profits are taken. Two new units are established with new expected moves.

*April 11, 2014*

| Status | Open/ Buy | Units | 1 | P/L | | Upper | 187.74 |
|--------|-----------|-------|---|-----|--|-------|--------|
| Date | 04/11/14 | Strike | 182/192 | Equity | 6,026.00 | Cost | 383.00 |
| SPY | 181.51 | Days | 70 | +/– | 6.23 | Initial BP | 4,166.00 |
| Exp | Jun 20 | Price | 383.00 | Lower | 175.28 | End BP | 3,783.00 |

The market moved sideways for a while, and then there was a small retracement which reached our lower limit expected move. Remember to always wait until 3:30 p.m. Eastern Time (1/2 hour before the markets close) to determine if the lower limit has been reached. Even if it has been reached during the trading day it may still go lower, or it may rally above the lower limit expected move. Since there are more than 45 days remaining until expiration we will use the same expiration date. One additional unit is established.

*April 22, 2014*

| Status | Close 1 | Units | | P/L | 244.00 | Upper | 193.40 |
|--------|---------|-------|--|-----|--------|-------|--------|
| Date | 04/22/14 | Strike | | Equity | 6,270.00 | Cost | |
| SPY | 187.89 | Days | 59 | +/− | 5.51 | Initial BP | 3,783.00 |
| Exp | Jun 20 | Price | | Lower | 182.38 | End BP | 4,410.00 |

The upper limit expected move has been reached. We close all units more than the initial two. Therefore we now close the last unit created on April 11, 2014. Since there are still 59 days remaining we will leave the other two units open. Remember that any time any positions are closed new expected moves will be created.

*May 21, 2014*

| Status | Close/ Buy | Units | 3 | P/L | −146.00 | Upper | 194.62 |
|--------|---------|-------|--|-----|--------|-------|--------|
| Date | 05/21/14 | Strike | 189/199 | Equity | 6,124.00 | Cost | 1,182.00 |
| SPY | 189.13 | Days | 121 | +/− | 5.49 | Initial BP | 4,854.00 |
| Exp | Sep 19 | Price | 394.00 | Lower | 183.64 | End BP | 3,672.00 |

Even though the upper expected move has not been reached, we are now 30 days from expiration and all positions must be closed regardless. As this was closed because of being 30 days from expiration and only two units were established we are going to open one additional unit with the new position.

Therefore three new units are established at the current level and new expected moves are created.

*June 6, 2014*

| Status | Close 1 | Units | | P/L | 207.00 | Upper | 199.72 |
|--------|---------|-------|--|-----|--------|-------|--------|
| Date | 06/06/14 | Strike | | Equity | 6,331.00 | Cost | |
| SPY | 195.38 | Days | 105 | +/− | 4.34 | Initial BP | 3,672.00 |
| Exp | Sep 19 | Price | | Lower | 191.04 | End BP | 4,273.00 |

The upper expected move has been reached. Since there are more than 45 days remaining only the last unit used to cover is closed leaving two units. The buying power is computed as one-third of the original cost and is restored plus the profit made.

*August 20, 2014*

| Status | Close/Buy | Units | 3 | P/L | 864.00 | Upper | 204.58 |
|---|---|---|---|---|---|---|---|
| Date | 08/20/14 | Strike | 199/210 | Equity | 7,195.00 | Cost | 1,116.00 |
| SPY | 198.92 | Days | 93 | +/– | 5.66 | Initial BP | 5,000.00 |
| Exp | Nov 21 | Price | 372.00 | Lower | 193.26 | End BP | 3,884.00 |

On August 7, 2014, the SPY actually officially closed one penny below the lower expected move. But this was a technical close which was not reported until a few minutes after the close of the market. Therefore there was no opportunity to add another position. The next day it opened above the lower limit so nothing was done.

On August 20, 2014, two things are occurring at once. First we are very close to the upper limit and second we are 30 days from expiration and would close all positions anyway. As this was technically closed because of being 30 days from expiration and only two units were established we are going to open one additional unit with the new position. Therefore three new units are established at the current level and new expected moves are created.

Notice that there is no 209 call strike. Therefore an 11-point spread is created with the 210 call strike.

*October 9, 2014*

| Status | Close/Buy | Units | 4 | P/L | –726.00 | Upper | 200.29 |
|---|---|---|---|---|---|---|---|
| Date | 10/09/14 | Strike | 193/203 | Equity | 6,469.00 | Cost | 1,788.00 |
| SPY | 192.74 | Days | 99 | +/– | 7.55 | Initial BP | 4,274.00 |
| Exp | Jan 16 | Price | 447.00 | Lower | 185.19 | End BP | 2,486.00 |

The lower expected move has been reached and one unit is added. Since we are less than 46 days from expiration all positions are closed and new positions are created. A four-unit position is established and new expected moves are created.

*October 31, 2014*

| Status | Close 2 | Units | | P/L | 490.00 | Upper | 207.87 |
|--------|---------|-------|---|-----|--------|-------|--------|
| Date | 10/31/14 | Strike | | Equity | 6,959.00 | Cost | 894.00 |
| SPY | 201.66 | Days | 77 | +/– | 6.21 | Initial BP | 2,486.00 |
| Exp | Nov 21 | Price | | Lower | 195.45 | End BP | 3,870.00 |

The upper expected move has been reached. Close two units. Remember you want to bring your position back to two units.

Let's recap what happened during the month of October 2014.

On October 13, 2014, the price of the SPY closed below the 200-day moving average. Now we looked to see the percentage distance the 50-day moving average was to the 200-day moving average. We see that it was well above the 1 percent threshold. Therefore we stayed in the market for the time being. We then started the five-day rule.

On the fifth trading day of the five-day rule the market rallied and even though the price of the SPY was still below the 200-day moving average, it was really close, and the price closed almost at the high of the day. As such a decision was made to stay in for one more trading day. If the next day was going to open lower all positions would be closed and trading suspended.

As it turned out it was a good decision that we decided to wait because the next day on October 21, 2014, the market gaped up substantially above the 200-day moving average. For the time being it looks like we are home free.

On October 31, the market rallied to the upper expected move and two units were closed out. When you have more than three units working you want to close out enough units to leave you with your initial two units.

## How Did We Do the First Year?

October 31, 2014, marks about one year since we began. Even though not all positions are closed out at this point, our closed out equity is

$6,959.00. That's a $1,959.00 increase and a 39.18 percent gain. It is much better than the S&P 500. Remember this is based on $5,000 available capital. The most that we had working at any one time was $2,514.00. During that same time frame the S&P 500 increased 14.44 percent. All of our goals were met.

*November 26, 2014*

| Status | Close/Buy | Units | 2 | P/L | 898.00 | Upper | 213.46 |
|--------|-----------|-------|-----|--------|----------|------------|----------|
| Date | 11/26/14 | Strike | 207/217 | Equity | 7,857.00 | Cost | 856.00 |
| SPY | 207.64 | Days | 113 | +/– | 5.82 | Initial BP | 5,000.00 |
| Exp | Mar 19 | Price | 428.00 | Lower | 201.82 | End BP | 4,144.00 |

The upper expected move has been reached. We are using the $0.75 option. The actual upper limit is 207.87. We closed at 207.64. Don't be a slave to pennies.

All positions are closed and profit taken. It may seem like the profit is excessive but remember this is a second upper expected move for these original two units. We started on October 9· with four units because first we reached 30 days from expiration level and we added the third unit. Then we reached a lower expected move and added the fourth unit. The market then rallied to an upper expected move and we close out our two cover units. So for these two initial units the market has gone from 192.74 to 207.64, about a 15-point gain. Also remember on October 9, we took a loss.

*December 12, 2014*

| Status | Open/Buy | Units | 1 | P/L | | Upper | 210.05 |
|--------|----------|-------|---------|--------|----------|------------|----------|
| Date | 12/12/14 | Strike | 200/210 | Equity | 7,857.00 | Cost | 470.00 |
| SPY | 200.89 | Days | 97 | +/– | 9.16 | Initial BP | 4,144.00 |
| Exp | Mar 19 | Price | 470.00 | Lower | 191.73 | End BP | 3,674.00 |

After such a large run-up the SPY had a retracement which caught our lower limit expected move. With 97 days remaining we're going to add one unit using the same expiration month. New expected moves are established.

### February 17, 2015

| Status | Close/Buy | Units | 2 | P/L | 438.00 | Upper | 218.30 |
|--------|-----------|-------|-----|--------|----------|------------|----------|
| Date | 02/17/15 | Strike | 210/220 | Equity | 8,295.00 | Cost | 940.00 |
| SPY | 210.11 | Days | 115 | +/– | 8.19 | Initial BP | 5,000.00 |
| Exp | Jun 19 | Price | 470.00 | Lower | 201.92 | End BP | 4,060.00 |

The upper limit expected move has been reached within our $0.75 limit. Since there are less than 46 days remaining all positions are closed and the profits are taken. Two new units are established with new expected moves.

### May 20, 2015

| Status | Close/Buy | Units | 3 | P/L | –70.00 | Upper | 219.49 |
|--------|-----------|-------|-----|--------|----------|------------|----------|
| Date | 05/20/15 | Strike | 213/223 | Equity | 8,225.00 | Cost | 1,215.00 |
| SPY | 212.88 | Days | 93 | +/– | 6.61 | Initial BP | 4,930.00 |
| Exp | Aug 21 | Price | 405.00 | Lower | 206.27 | End BP | 3,715.00 |

We are now 30 days out from expiration and all units must be closed. Since we only have two units then one unit will be added. Three units are now established at the new price level. New expected moves are established. The $70.00 loss is subtracted from the $5,000.00 initial buying power to reflect the new initial buying power.

### June 29, 2015

| Status | Open/Buy | Units | 1 | P/L | | Upper | 214.24 |
|--------|-----------|-------|-----|--------|----------|------------|----------|
| Date | 06/29/15 | Strike | 206/216 | Equity | 8,225.00 | Cost | 420.00 |
| SPY | 205.42 | Days | 53 | +/– | 8.82 | Initial BP | 3,715.00 |
| Exp | Aug 21 | Price | 420.00 | Lower | 196.60 | End BP | 3,295.00 |

The market had been absolutely flat over the last two months. It finally dropped below the lower expected move. One new position was created giving us a total of four units, and new expected moves are established.

*July 22, 2015*

| Status | Close/ Buy | Units | 4 | P/L | −562.00 | Upper | 217.23 |
|--------|------------|-------|-----|------|---------|-----------|----------|
| Date | 07/22/15 | Strike | 211/221 | Equity | 7,663.00 | Cost | 1,856.00 |
| SPY | 211.37 | Days | 93 | +/− | 5.86 | Initial BP | 4,368.00 |
| Exp | Nov 20 | Price | 464.00 | Lower | 205.51 | End BP | 2,512.00 |

We are now 30 days out from expiration and all units are closed. Since we already have four units we do not add any more because of expiration. Four units are established and new expected moves are established.

Remember if you have three units established because you have previously reached a lower limit and have never added a unit because of expiration then you may add one more unit bringing your total to four. Under no circumstances add a unit because of expiration if you already have four units established regardless of the reason they were added.

*August 20, 2015*

| Status | Close All | Units | | P/L | −1,010.00 | Upper | |
|--------|-----------|-------|--|--------|-----------|-----------|----------|
| Date | 08/20/15 | Strike | | Equity | 6,653.00 | Cost | |
| SPY | 206.46 | Days | | +/− | | Initial BP | 4,368.00 |
| Exp | | Price | | Lower | | End BP | 3,358.00 |

Today, August 20, 2015, the price of the SPY dipped below the 200-day moving average. When we look at where the 50-day moving average is we see that it is less than 1 percent of the 200-day moving average. Therefore we are not going to use the five-day rule, and we're going to close all positions immediately. Notice that if the 50-day moving average is <1 percent of the 200-day moving average, the price by 3:30 p.m. Eastern Time only has to close below the 200-day moving average by any amount, not by a substantial amount.

Now that all positions are forced closed we cannot reenter the market until either we cross back above the 200-day moving average followed by the five-day rule or, after a correction, we cross back above the 50-day moving average whichever is lower, and again applying the five-day rule. The 50-day moving average after a correction should be below the 200-day moving average.

For the time being we are completely out of the market. We are not trying to predict where the market is going. According to our rules the market is just too dangerous at this point.

*October 15, 2015*

| Status | Open/Buy | Units | 5 | P/L | | Upper | 209.31 |
|---|---|---|---|---|---|---|---|
| Date | 10/15/15 | Strike | 202/212 | Equity | 6,653.00 | Cost | 2,330.00 |
| SPY | 202.18 | Days | 92 | +/– | 7.13 | Initial BP | 3,358.00 |
| Exp | Jan 15 | Price | 466.00 | Lower | 195.05 | End BP | 1,028.00 |

Wow! It's a good thing we got out of the market when we did. It took a wild ride all the way down to a low on the SPY of 182. Volatility increased tremendously. This lasted for a little less than a month. On October 7, 2015, the SPY closed above the 50-day moving average which is by now well below the 200-day moving average.

We then waited the five trading days according to the five-day rule. October 14, 2015, was the fifth day. That was a down day and the SPY did not close above the top of the body of the candle of the trigger day which was October 7. So we could not reenter at that point.

The next trading day, October 15, 2015, the SPY closed above the 50-day moving average. At this point we're using the rolling five-day rule. This means that we looked back five trading days and we saw that on October 8, 2015, the SPY also closed above the 50-day moving average as it had done the day before. Therefore since five days later on October 15, 2015, the SPY is now above the top of the body of the candle of the new trigger day which was October 8, we are permitted to reenter the market.

The next thing we do is to see where the last lower limit expected move was. It was at 205.51. We are now at 202.18. Since we are below the last lower limit we are going to reenter the market with one additional unit from what we had when we closed which was four units. We now reenter the market with five units. New expected moves are established.

*November 2, 2015*

| Status | Close All | Units | | P/L | 1,147.00 | Upper | |
|---|---|---|---|---|---|---|---|
| Date | 11/02/15 | Strike | | Equity | 7,800.00 | Cost | |
| SPY | 210.39 | Days | | +/– | | Initial BP | 3,358.00 |
| Exp | | Price | | Lower | | End BP | 4,505.00 |

The market rallied and on November 2, 2015, the upper limit expected move was reached. All positions are closed. The reason that all positions are closed rather than just the three units is because this is the first successful trade after being forced out of the market. You are permitted one successful trade after you reenter the market when the 50-day moving average is below the 1 percent level of the 200-day moving average. After that one trade when the upper expected move has been reached you must stay out of the market until such time as the 50-day moving average is ≥1 percent above the 200-day moving average.

At this point according to the rules, all trading is suspended until such time as the 50-day moving average is above the 200-day moving average by 1 percent or more.

Another thing to note, since the previous buying power was $3,358, and $1,147 profit was added, we're are not back to $5,000. Therefore the current buying power is only $4,505.

## How Did We Do the Second Year?

It's November 2, 2015, two years after we began, and our equity stands at $7,800. During the second year we made $841. This is a 16.82 percent gain. This is exceptional when you consider how flat the S&P 500 was during 2015. Our two-year average gain per year is 28 percent. We definitely met our goals. Even though we did not reach the 20 percent level for the year, we did almost four times better than the S&P 500. Its gain for the year was only 4.33 percent and its average yearly gain for the two-year period was only 9.39 percent.

*March 3, 2016*

| Status | Open/ Buy | Units | 2 | P/L | | Upper | 207.27 |
|---|---|---|---|---|---|---|---|
| Date | 03/03/16 | Strike | 199/209 | Equity | 7,800.00 | Cost | 948.00 |
| SPY | 199.78 | Days | 106 | +/– | 7.49 | Initial BP | 4,505.00 |
| Exp | Jun 17 | Price | 474.00 | Lower | 192.29 | End BP | 3,557.00 |

This is a prime example of the wisdom of waiting after the first reentry following a correction until the 50-day moving average is ≥1 percent above the 200-day moving average. For four months the price of the SPY meandered above and below the 200-day moving average. The 50-day moving average never even got above the 200-day moving average. We would have been whipsawed. During this time there was even a major correction to the downside which we avoided.

When we look at the chart on March 3, 2016, we see that the 50-day moving average is still below the 200-day moving average. But one thing is now different. During that time there was another major correction and now the price of the SPY has rallied above the 50-day moving average for the second time after that correction.

Because of that major correction we can now take advantage of the second crossover of the 50-day moving average by the SPY. This occurred on February 22, 2016. Using the five-day rule we look at the close on February 29, 2016, and find that it is below the top of the candle body of the trigger day which was February 22. As such we do not reenter the market at this point. Using the rolling five-day rule, the next time the SPY closed above the 50-day moving average was on February 25, 2016. Again we apply the five-day rule and on March 3, 2016, the SPY closed above the top of the body of the candle of the new trigger day which was February 25. We are now ready to reenter the market.

We enter with two units and establish new expected moves. We do not add a unit because our last trade reached the upper expected move.

*April 1, 2016*

| Status | Close All | Units | | P/L | 436.00 | Upper | |
|---|---|---|---|---|---|---|---|
| Date | 04/01/16 | Strike | | Equity | 8,236.00 | Cost | |
| SPY | 206.92 | Days | | +/– | | Initial BP | 4,505.00 |
| Exp | | Price | | Lower | | End BP | 4,941.00 |

The upper limit of the expected move is reached within our $0.75 limit. The actual upper limit was 207.27 and we closed at 206.92. All positions are closed. As before we look to see if the 50-day moving average is above the 200-day moving average by 1 percent or more. It is not as yet. As a result we will suspend all trading until such time as the 50-day moving average is ≥1 percent above the 200-day moving average unless there is another major correction. Remember since the last trade was to reenter the market it is a one and done.

*April 27, 2016*

| Status | Open/ Buy | Units | 2 | P/L | | Upper | 215.93 |
|---|---|---|---|---|---|---|---|
| Date | 04/27/16 | Strike | 209/219 | Equity | 8,236.00 | Cost | 958.00 |
| SPY | 209.35 | Days | 114 | +/– | 6.58 | Initial BP | 4,941.00 |
| Exp | Aug 19 | Price | 479.00 | Lower | 202.77 | End BP | 3,983.00 |

The 50-day moving average is now greater than 1 percent above the 200-day moving average and it is time to reenter the market. We reenter with two units and establish new expected moves.

*June 27, 2016*

| Status | Open/ Buy | Units | 1 | P/L | | Upper | 210.31 |
|---|---|---|---|---|---|---|---|
| Date | 06/27/16 | Strike | 200/210 | Equity | 8,236.00 | Cost | 438.00 |
| SPY | 199.60 | Days | 52 | +/– | 10.71 | Initial BP | 3,983.00 |
| Exp | Aug 18 | Price | 438.00 | Lower | 188.89 | End BP | 3,545.00 |

On June 27, 2016, the lower limit expected move was reached. But the SPY also crossed below the 200-day moving average which would start the five-day rule. Remember that the expected move tends to add a floor to a downward move. And a single dip below the 200-day moving average is not that significant. That is the reason for the five-day rule. Therefore it is OK to go ahead and add one unit as you normally would. The next day the SPY crossed back above the 200-day moving average.

*July 1, 2016*

| Status | Close 1 | Units | | P/L | 327.00 | Upper | 216.59 |
|--------|---------|-------|---|-----|--------|-------|--------|
| Date | 07/01/16 | Strike | | Equity | 8,563.00 | Cost | |
| SPY | 209.92 | Days | 49 | +/– | 6.67 | Initial BP | 3,545.00 |
| Exp | Aug 19 | Price | | Lower | 203.25 | End BP | 4,310.00 |

The upper limit was reached within $0.75. The last one unit cover was closed and new expected moves established.

*July 14, 2016*

| Status | Close/ Buy | Units | 2 | P/L | 394.00 | Upper | 222.24 |
|--------|-----------|-------|---|-----|--------|-------|--------|
| Date | 07/14/16 | Strike | 216/226 | Equity | 8,957.00 | Cost | 842.00 |
| SPY | 216.12 | Days | 99 | +/– | 6.12 | Initial BP | 5,000.00 |
| Exp | Oct 21 | Price | 421.00 | Lower | 210.00 | End BP | 4,158.00 |

The upper limit expected move was reached and all positions closed. Two new units were purchased and expected moves established. Remember that the $0.75 option is just that, an option. This is a perfect time to use that option. It is only $0.47 from the actual expected move, but more importantly there are only 36 days remaining until expiration. In a few days you would have to close anyway.

*September 21, 2016*

| Status | Close/ Buy | Units | 3 | P/L | –268.00 | Upper | 222.51 |
|--------|-----------|-------|---|-----|---------|-------|--------|
| Date | 09/21/16 | Strike | 215/225 | Equity | 8,689.00 | Cost | 1,548.00 |
| SPY | 215.82 | Days | 100 | +/– | 6.69 | Initial BP | 4,732.00 |
| Exp | Dec 30 | Price | 516.00 | Lower | 209.13 | End BP | 3,184.00 |

None of the expected moves has been reached, but we are now 30 days until expiration and must close all positions. One position is added. Three new positions are being established at the current level with new expected moves. Even though we should have used the 216/226 spread, there was no 226 strike price. So to keep a 10-point spread the 215/225 spread was used.

*November 3, 2016*

| Status | Open/ Buy | Units | 1 | P/L | | Upper | 218.33 |
|---|---|---|---|---|---|---|---|
| Date | 11/03/16 | Strike | 209/219 | Equity | 8,689.00 | Cost | 437.00 |
| SPY | 208.78 | Days | 57 | +/– | 9.55 | Initial BP | 3,184.00 |
| Exp | Dec 30 | Price | 437.00 | Lower | 199.23 | End BP | 2,747.00 |

The presidential election is in a few days on November 8, 2016, and the SPY took a dip and caught the lower limit expected move. Because there are 57 days remaining until expiration we will use the same expiration month and purchase one unit to cover, establishing new expected moves. We now have four units working.

*November 15, 2016*

| Status | Close/ Buy | Units | 2 | P/L | 242.00 | Upper | 224.69 |
|---|---|---|---|---|---|---|---|
| Date | 11/15/16 | Strike | 218/228 | Equity | 8,931.00 | Cost | 878.00 |
| SPY | 218.28 | Days | 94 | +/– | 6.41 | Initial BP | 4,974.00 |
| Exp | Feb 17 | Price | 439.00 | Lower | 211.87 | End BP | 4,096.00 |

Following the presidential election the market rallied to the upper limit expected move. There are 45 days remaining. Since we have <46 days all positions are closed and two new units are established with new expected moves. Note that when you created the expected moves you had a choice between expirations that were 31 days and 29 days. Since these are the same distance from 30 you may choose either one. I prefer to choose the 29 since it will give me a lower upper limit and as such is more conservative.

## How Did We Do the Third Year?

We ended the year with an equity of $8,931. This was a gain of $1,131. This is a 22.62 percent increase for the year. The three-year yearly average is now 26.21 percent. The S&P 500 had a gain of 3.75 percent for the year and a three-year average gain of only 7.51 percent per year. We achieved all of our goals.

*December 8, 2016*

| Status | Close/Buy | Units | 2 | P/L | 393.00 | Upper | 231.37 |
|--------|-----------|-------|-----|------|--------|------------|----------|
| Date | 12/08/16 | Strike | 225/235 | Equity | 9,324.00 | Cost | 842.00 |
| SPY | 225.15 | Days | 99 | +/– | 6.22 | Initial BP | 5,000.00 |
| Exp | Mar 17 | Price | 421.00 | Lower | 218.93 | End BP | 4,158.00 |

The upper limit has been reached. All positions are closed. Two new units are established at the current level and the new expected moves are created.

*February 10, 2017*

| Status | Close/Buy | Units | 2 | P/L | 456.00 | Upper | 236.83 |
|--------|-----------|-------|-----|------|--------|------------|----------|
| Date | 02/10/17 | Strike | 232/242 | Equity | 9,780.00 | Cost | 796.00 |
| SPY | 231.51 | Days | 99 | +/– | 5.32 | Initial BP | 5,000.00 |
| Exp | May 19 | Price | 398.00 | Lower | 226.19 | End BP | 4,204.00 |

The upper limit has been reached using the 20 percent to 25 percent or more profit option. All positions are closed. Two new units are established at the current level and the new expected moves are created.

*February 21, 2017*

| Status | Close/Buy | Units | 2 | P/L | 316.00 | Upper | 242.55 |
|--------|-----------|-------|-----|------|--------|------------|----------|
| Date | 02/21/17 | Strike | 236/246 | Equity | 10,096.00 | Cost | 890.00 |
| SPY | 236.49 | Days | 115 | +/– | 6.06 | Initial BP | 5,000.00 |
| Exp | Jun 16 | Price | 445.00 | Lower | 230.43 | End BP | 4,110.00 |

The upper limit has been reached within $0.75. All positions are closed. Two new units are established at the current level and the new expected moves are created. Again I've chosen the 29-day expected move over the 31-day expected move.

*May 17, 2017*

| Status | Close/ Buy | Units | 3 | P/L | –252.00 | Upper | 244.63 |
|--------|-----------|-------|--------|------|---------|-----------|----------|
| Date | 05/17/17 | Strike | 236/246 | Equity | 9,844.00 | Cost | 1,362.00 |
| SPY | 235.82 | Days | 93 | +/– | 8.81 | Initial BP | 4,748.00 |
| Exp | Aug 18 | Price | 454.00 | Lower | 227.01 | End BP | 3,386.00 |

There are now 30 days remaining until expiration and all positions are closed. One position is added and three new positions are established and new expected moves created.

*June 2, 2017*

| Status | Close 1 | Units | | P/L | 248.00 | Upper | 249.47 |
|--------|---------|-------|----|------|----------|-----------|----------|
| Date | 06/02/17 | Strike | | Equity | 10,092.00 | Cost | |
| SPY | 244.17 | Days | 77 | +/– | 5.30 | Initial BP | 3,386.00 |
| Exp | Aug 18 | Price | | Lower | 238.87 | End BP | 4,088.00 |

The upper limit has been reached within $0.75. One unit is closed. There are more than 45 days remaining until expiration. The original two units remain intact. New expected moves are created.

*July 19, 2017*

| Status | Close/ Buy | Units | 3 | P/L | 851.00 | Upper | 252.56 |
|--------|-----------|-------|--------|------|-----------|-----------|----------|
| Date | 07/19/17 | Strike | 247/257 | Equity | 10,943.00 | Cost | 1,206.00 |
| SPY | 246.99 | Days | 98 | +/– | 5.57 | Initial BP | 5,000.00 |
| Exp | Oct 20 | Price | 402.00 | Lower | 241.42 | End BP | 3,794.00 |

There are 30 days until expiration and all positions are closed. One unit is added. Three new positions are established and new upper and lower expected moves are created.

*September 20, 2017*

| Status | Close/ Buy | Units | 3 | P/L | 114.00 | Upper | 255.74 |
|--------|-----------|-------|-----|-------|----------|-----------|----------|
| Date | 09/20/17 | Strike | 250/260 | Equity | 11,057.00 | Cost | 1,374.00 |
| SPY | 250.06 | Days | 100 | +/– | 5.68 | Initial BP | 5,000.00 |
| Exp | Dec 29 | Price | 458.00 | Lower | 244.38 | End BP | 3,626.00 |

There are 30 days remaining until expiration and all positions are closed. The same three positions are created. A new position is not added since one has already been added on July 19, because of being 30 days from expiration. You do not add a unit because of being 30 days from expiration if one has already been added for that reason. You are permitted to add one unit because of being 30 days from expiration if this is the first time a unit has been added for that reason. In this case we already have a unit added because of expiration.

Even though the put bid is not greater than the call ask, you do not go up to the next higher level since it is not a $1.00 increase, but a $5.00 increase in this expiration period. Therefore it is better to stay as close to the At the Money as possible. So the 250 strike is chosen.

*October 16, 2017*

| Status | Close 1 | Units | | P/L | 189.00 | Upper | 260.83 |
|--------|---------|-------|-----|-------|----------|-----------|----------|
| Date | 10/16/17 | Strike | | Equity | 11,246.00 | Cost | |
| SPY | 255.29 | Days | 74 | +/– | 5.54 | Initial BP | 3,626.00 |
| Exp | Dec 29 | Price | | Lower | 249.75 | End BP | 4,273.00 |

The upper limit has been reached and one unit is closed. The one that is closed is the cover unit. New expected moves are established.

## How Did We Do the Fourth Year?

This was an extremely easy year. Our ending equity was $11,246.00. It seemed like nothing could go wrong. Our gain was $2,315.00. This was a 46.30 percent increase. The average yearly return for the four years is

31.23 percent. The S&P 500 gained 16.96 percent for the year and its average yearly return for the four years was only 9.87 percent.

*November 24, 2017*

| Status | Close/ Buy | Units | 2 | P/L | 800.00 | Upper | 265.90 |
|--------|-----------|-------|---|-----|--------|-------|--------|
| Date | 11/24/17 | Strike | 260/270 | Equity | 12,046.00 | Cost | 910.00 |
| SPY | 260.36 | Days | 112 | +/− | 5.54 | Initial BP | 5,000.00 |
| Exp | Mar 16 | Price | 455.00 | Lower | 254.82 | End BP | 4,090.00 |

The upper limit has been reached within $0.75 and all positions closed. Two new positions are created and new expected moves established.

*December 8, 2017*

| Status | Close/ Buy | Units | 2 | P/L | 387.00 | Upper | 270.90 |
|--------|-----------|-------|---|-----|--------|-------|--------|
| Date | 12/08/17 | Strike | 265/275 | Equity | 12,433.00 | Cost | 916.00 |
| SPY | 265.51 | Days | 98 | +/− | 5.39 | Initial BP | 5,000.00 |
| Exp | Mar 16 | Price | 458.00 | Lower | 260.12 | End BP | 4,084.00 |

The upper limit of the expected move was reached. Two new positions were created and new expected moves were established. Even though we should have had a spread from 266 to 276, there was no 276 strike available so we went with the 265 to 275 spread.

*January 3, 2018*

| Status | Close/ Buy | Units | 2 | P/L | 401.00 | Upper | 275.99 |
|--------|-----------|-------|---|-----|--------|-------|--------|
| Date | 01/03/18 | Strike | 270/280 | Equity | 12,834.00 | Cost | 962.00 |
| SPY | 270.47 | Days | 107 | +/− | 5.52 | Initial BP | 5,000.00 |
| Exp | Apr 20 | Price | 481.00 | Lower | 264.95 | End BP | 4,038.00 |

The upper limit of the expected move was reached. Two new positions were created and new expected moves were established. Again we should be using the 271 to 281 spread, but there is no 281 strike so we will use the 270 to 280 spread.

*January 11, 2018*

| Status | Close/Buy | Units | 2 | P/L | 363.00 | Upper | 282.06 |
|--------|-----------|-------|---|-----|--------|-------|--------|
| Date | 01/11/18 | Strike | 276/285 | Equity | 13,197.00 | Cost | 830.00 |
| SPY | 276.12 | Days | 99 | +/– | 5.97 | Initial BP | 5,000.00 |
| Exp | Apr 20 | Price | 415.00 | Lower | 270.15 | End BP | 4,170.00 |

The upper limit of the expected move was reached. Two new positions were created and new expected moves were established. Another adjustment in the strikes needed to be made. There was no 287 call strike available. And using the 275 strike would have put us too far In the Money for a beginning strike. Therefore the 276 and 285 call strikes were chosen even though it is only a 9-point spread.

*January 22, 2018*

| Status | Close/Buy | Units | 2 | P/L | 407.00 | Upper | 289.76 |
|--------|-----------|-------|---|-----|--------|-------|--------|
| Date | 01/22/18 | Strike | 283/293 | Equity | 13,604.00 | Cost | 966.00 |
| SPY | 282.69 | Days | 116 | +/– | 7.07 | Initial BP | 5,000.00 |
| Exp | May 18 | Price | 483.00 | Lower | 275.62 | End BP | 4,034.00 |

The upper limit of the expected move was reached. Two new positions were created and new expected moves were established.

*February 2, 2018*

| Status | Open/Buy | Units | 1 | P/L | | Upper | 285.39 |
|--------|----------|-------|---|-----|--|-------|--------|
| Date | 02/02/18 | Strike | 276/286 | Equity | 13,604.00 | Cost | 508.00 |
| SPY | 275.45 | Days | 105 | +/– | 9.94 | Initial BP | 4,034.00 |
| Exp | May 18 | Price | 508.00 | Lower | 264.51 | End BP | 3,526.00 |

The lower limit expected move was reached. Since there are 105 days remaining we will use the same expiration month as before. One additional unit is purchased and new expected moves are established.

*February 5, 2018*

| Status | Open/ Buy | Units | 1 | P/L | | Upper | 282.95 |
|--------|-----------|-------|---|-----|---|-------|--------|
| Date | 02/05/18 | Strike | 264/274 | Equity | 13,604.00 | Cost | 531.00 |
| SPY | 263.93 | Days | 102 | +/– | 19.02 | Initial BP | 3,526.00 |
| Exp | May 18 | Price | 531.00 | Lower | 244.91 | End BP | 2,995.00 |

This is the first major down move for quite a while. The next day the SPY dipped impressively below the 50-day moving average but is still substantially above the 200-day moving average. In addition the 50-day moving average is well above the 1 percent level of the 200-day moving average. Since we closed below our lower limit we will add one more unit to our position and establish new expected moves. We now have four units.

This is the first time in our tutorial that the lower limit has been breached twice in a row. Notice how the range of the expected move is increasing dramatically. This is because volatility is increasing. Notice also at this point how our mathematical model makes it impossible to have a third lower limit in a row breached since that would be below our 200-day moving average. As such, if we got down that far we would be forced out of the market before we would have to add another unit. This is the nature of the system to prevent you from trying to catch a falling knife.

*April 18, 2018*

| Status | Close/ Buy | Units | 4 | P/L | –1,175.00 | Upper | 280.15 |
|--------|-----------|-------|---|-----|-----------|-------|--------|
| Date | 04/18/18 | Strike | 271/281 | Equity | 12,429.00 | Cost | 1,872.00 |
| SPY | 270.39 | Days | 93 | +/– | 9.76 | Initial BP | 3,825.00 |
| Exp | Jul 20 | Price | 468.00 | Lower | 260.63 | End BP | 1,953.00 |

On February 9, 2018, the SPY dipped briefly below the 200-day moving average but closed above. As such our five-day count was not put in effect. On March 23, 2018, the SPY did close a little below the 200-day moving average. But you would not call that substantial so we did not begin the five-day rule. Again on April 2, 2018, there was another close below the 200-day moving average. But as before it was not substantial so we did not begin the five-day rule. The market did continue to rally until April 18, 2018, when we were forced to close all of the positions since we are now 30 days from expiration.

All positions were closed and since we already had four units open we did not add an additional unit because of expiration. Even with four units open, if the SPY had fallen to the lower limit then one additional unit would have been added. It is only for expiration that we have any rules about not adding additional units. Remember do not add an additional unit because of being 30 days from expiration when you already have four units established even if you have never added a unit because of expiration. Four units were opened. New expected moves were established.

## June 20, 2018

| Status | Close/ Buy | Units | 4 | P/L | 610.00 | Upper | 284.09 |
|--------|-----------|--------|---------|--------|-----------|------------|----------|
| Date | 06/20/18 | Strike | 276/286 | Equity | 13,039.00 | Cost | 2,060.00 |
| SPY | 275.97 | Days | 93 | +/− | 8.12 | Initial BP | 4,435.00 |
| Exp | Sep 21 | Price | 515.00 | Lower | 267.85 | End BP | 2,375.00 |

We still have not reached the upper limit of the expected move but we are now 30 days from expiration and must close all four positions. Since we already had four units open we did not add an additional unit. Four new positions were opened at the new level and new expected moves were created.

## July 25, 2018

| Status | Close 2 | Units | | P/L | 423.00 | Upper | 291.73 |
|--------|---------|--------|-----|--------|-----------|------------|----------|
| Date | 07/25/18 | Strike | | Equity | 13,462.00 | Cost | |
| SPY | 284.01 | Days | 58 | +/− | 7.72 | Initial BP | 2,375.00 |
| Exp | Sep 21 | Price | | Lower | 276.29 | End BP | 3,828.00 |

The upper expected move has been reached. Since there are more than 45 days remaining until expiration we will close only two units. This will bring us back to our base of two units. All units are the same from the June 20, 2018, position. Another interesting thing to note is that you never know when a big rally will begin.

*August 22, 2018*

| Status | Close/ Buy | Units | 3 | P/L | 614.00 | Upper | 294.58 |
|--------|------------|-------|---|-----|--------|-------|--------|
| Date | 08/22/18 | Strike | 287/297 | Equity | 14,076.00 | Cost | 1,467.00 |
| SPY | 286.17 | Days | 121 | +/– | 8.41 | Initial BP | 5,000.00 |
| Exp | Dec 21 | Price | 489.00 | Lower | 277.76 | End BP | 3,533.00 |

We reached 30 days prior to expiration. All positions are closed and one additional unit is added giving us three units. New expected moves are established.

*September 20, 2018*

| Status | Close 1 | Units | | P/L | 180.00 | Upper | 301.46 |
|--------|---------|-------|---|-----|--------|-------|--------|
| Date | 09/20/18 | Strike | | Equity | 14,256.00 | Cost | |
| SPY | 293.58 | Days | 92 | +/– | 7.88 | Initial BP | 3,533.00 |
| Exp | Dec 21 | Price | | Lower | 285.70 | End BP | 4,202.00 |

The SPY made a high of 293.94 and as such it reached the upper limit within $0.75. The one cover unit is closed leaving the two original units. New expected moves are established.

*October 10, 2018*

| Status | Open/ Buy | Units | 1 | P/L | | Upper | 291.37 |
|--------|-----------|-------|---|-----|---|-------|--------|
| Date | 10/10/18 | Strike | 278/288 | Equity | 14,256.00 | Cost | 526.00 |
| SPY | 278.30 | Days | 72 | +/– | 13.07 | Initial BP | 4,202.00 |
| Exp | Dec 21 | Price | 526.00 | Lower | 265.23 | End BP | 3,676.00 |

On October 10, 2018, the SPY closed below the lower limit on a big move. One unit was added.

*October 18, 2018*

| Status | Close All | Units | | P/L | −616.00 | Upper | |
|--------|-----------|-------|---|-----|---------|-------|---|
| Date | 10/18/18 | Strike | | Equity | 13,640.00 | Cost | |
| SPY | 276.40 | Days | | +/− | | Initial BP | 5,000.00 |
| Exp | | Price | | Lower | | End BP | 4,384.00 |

On October 11, 2018, there was a substantial move below the 200-day moving average. Because the 50-day moving average was more than 1 percent above the 200-day moving average the five-day rule began. On the fifth trading day, October 18, 2018, the SPY closed below the 200-day moving average and all positions were closed. This was to be the beginning of one of the largest corrections since 2007 and we are out.

On November 7, 2018, there was a substantial move above the 200-day moving average generating the five-day rule on the upside. This didn't last long as there was another substantial pullback below the 200-day moving average so we will stay out of the market.

On December 3, 2018, the market closed again substantially above the 200-day moving average. We began the five-day rule but again there was a dramatic move to the downside in the SPY. Therefore we are still out of the market.

Notice that each time the market tries a rally above the 200-day moving average the five-day rule saves us as each rally fails. The market then had a severe correction.

On January 17, 2019, the SPY finally closed substantially above the 50-day moving average. The five-day rule on the upside is now in effect.

## How Did We Do the Fifth Year?

The year 2018 looked like it was going to be a pretty good year until October 11, 2018. That was the beginning of a major correction. Fortunately our system got us out on October 18, 2018, before too much damage was done.

For our fiscal year November 2017 to November 2018 our system gained $2,394 or 47.88 percent. Our overall five-year average yearly return is 34.56 percent. The S&P 500 during this same November to November time period gained only 6 percent and its average yearly return over five years is only 12.16 percent.

But this does not tell the whole story for 2018. The worst was yet to come for the S&P 500.

We were out of the market for the remainder of the calendar year. But the S&P 500 continued to lose money. For the calendar year 2018 the S&P 500 lost 7.6 percent while at the same time our gain for the calendar year was a very impressive 21.74 percent. Even for this really tough year we reached our goal of at least a 20 percent return for the year whether you measure from our fiscal year or calendar year. And of course it was a much better performance than the loss that the S&P 500 suffered.

## What Happened after the Major Correction of 2018?

*January 25, 2019*

| Status | Open/ Buy | Units | 3 | P/L | | Upper | 275.94 |
|--------|-----------|-------|-----|-----|------------|------------|----------|
| Date | 01/25/19 | Strike | 266/276 | Equity | 13,640.00 | Cost | 1,560.00 |
| SPY | 265.78 | Days | 112 | +/– | 10.16 | Initial BP | 4,384.00 |
| Exp | May 17 | Price | 520.00 | Lower | 255.62 | End BP | 2,824.00 |

We were out of the market during most of the severe correction at the end of 2018. That is why we were able to post a gain of more than 20 percent for the calendar year while the S&P 500 posted a loss.

The market finally reached its bottom on December 26, 2018. The low point for the SPY was 234.27. From there the market made a steady climb over the next three weeks and the price of the SPY decisively crossed the 50-day moving average on January 17, 2019.

At this point our procedure is to wait five trading days to see if the SPY is above the top of the candle body of the trigger day which was January 17. On January 25, 2019, the SPY closed above the top of the body of the trigger day and as such we reentered the market.

*February 15, 2019*

| Status | Close All | Units | | P/L | 619.00 | Upper | |
|--------|-----------|-------|-----|-----|-----------|------------|----------|
| Date | 02/15/19 | Strike | | Equity | 14,259.00 | Cost | |
| SPY | 277.39 | Days | | +/– | | Initial BP | 4,384.00 |
| Exp | | Price | | Lower | | End BP | 5,000.00 |

The upper limit expected move was reached on February 15, 2019. We exited the position with a $619 profit.

Our trading is now suspended until such time as the 50-day moving average moves above the 200-day moving average by 1 percent.

The 50-day moving average moved above the 200-day moving average by 1 percent on April 10, 2019. At that point we reentered the market. Our total gain for calendar year 2019 was $2,417 which was a gain of 48.34 percent. The S&P 500 also had a good year. In 2019 virtually nothing could go wrong. The S&P 500 gained 22.27 percent.

As you can see these five years of trading have provided virtually every scenario that you can imagine, both good and bad, and The Non-Timing Trading System performed as it was designed. With a rules-based system you are not trying to time the market. You are letting the market tell you what to do. Emotions are removed from the equation. That is why The Non-Timing Trading System will consistently give you 20 percent to 30 percent returns year after year.

## What Happened in 2020 with the Covid-19 Crash?

The year 2020 began as a very good year continuing the way 2019 ended. Then on February 20, 2020, everything went horribly wrong. In a matter of a one-month period the SPY went from a high of 339.08 on February 19 to a low of 218.26 on March 23. We exited the market on March 5, 2020, with the SPY at 302.

We were out of the market until the SPY crossed the 50-day moving average and satisfied the five-day rule on April 27, 2020. We reentered the market and exited when the upper limit was reached. The loss incurred from the forced exit on March 5th was almost completely recovered with this one trade.

As of December 9, 2020, our total gain for the calendar year 2020 is $1,824.00. That is a 36.48 percent gain for the year so far. The S&P 500 has gained 14.34 percent for the calendar year as of December 9, 2020.

# CHAPTER 9

# Analysis

## Draw Downs

Our definition of a draw down is the lowest amount of buying power available at any time. This is computed after a close out and the next establishment of another position. It will occur after a loss or series of losses minus the capital used to establish the next position.

The following is a chart for each year listing the largest draw down and the buying power remaining.

| Year | Date | Draw Down | Buying Power |
|------|------|-----------|--------------|
| 1 | 10/9/14 | 2,514.00 | 2,486.00 |
| 2 | 10/15/15 | 3,972.00 | 1,028.00 |
| 3 | 11/3/16 | 2,253.00 | 2,747.00 |
| 4 | 5/17/17 | 1,614.00 | 3,386.00 |
| 5 | 4/18/18 | 3,047.00 | 1,953.00 |

## Largest Loss

At any closing of positions this is the largest loss incurred for the year and the resulting buying power available is after the loss is subtracted from either the initial $5,000 capital or the previous buying power whichever is lower. The actual loss on any given day is not computed since the positions are not closed. This means that when a lower limit is reached the paper loss at that time might be more than what is listed below. But since the position was not closed it was not calculated.

| Year | Date | Loss | Buying Power |
|------|------|------|--------------|
| 1 | 10/9/14 | 726.00 | 4,274.00 |
| 2 | 8/20/15 | 1,010.00 | 3,358.00 |
| 3 | 9/21/16 | 268.00 | 4,732.00 |
| 4 | 5/17/17 | 252.00 | 4,748.00 |
| 5 | 4/18/18 | 1,175.00 | 3,825.00 |

## How Does the System Work in the Long Term?

Five years should be a substantial amount of time to test a system. But let's face it, the market has been in a bull market since March 9, 2009. From the low of March 9, 2009, until March 9, 2019, the SPY went from 68.11 to 274.46. That's a 403 percent increase in 10 years or an average of 40 percent per year. Obviously a buy-and-hold strategy for those 10 years would have grown $5,000 to $20,150 not accounting for any compounding.

The problem with this assumption is that you would have to have known that on March 9, 2009, the bear market had come to an end and that there would be a 10-year bull market. If you look at the previous 10 years on March 9, 1999, the market closed at 128.06. A buy-and-hold strategy would have lost 46.82 percent, more than half the capital. That is an average loss of almost 5 percent per year. Your $5,000 would have decreased to $2,659. Again this is not accounting for any compounding. You would not have been back to break even until January 12, 2011, 12 years later, a 22-year round trip.

The point is not the actual numbers, but the fact that any time from March 9, 2009, you probably could have made money in the stock market no matter what long system you were using. Obviously the major bear market of 2007 to 2009 devastated most portfolios. So let's see how The Non-Timing Trading System would have done prior to and through the bear market. We will go back 15 years and begin our study on March 9, 2004.

For this study we are not interested in how much money we would make when the market is going up. We have already shown that The Non-Timing Trading System can outperform the S&P 500 when the market goes up. What we are interested in is how the system handles downturns, especially the bear market of 2007.

Therefore the key dates that we will focus on are the beginnings of downturns and reentries into the market. It would be very helpful if you follow along with a chart to see visually what was happening on the dates as you read the explanations.

On **March 9, 2004**, the SPY was at 114.50. This was above the 50-day and 200-day moving averages.

**May 10, 2004:** The SPY approaches the 200-day moving average but does not close below it.

**July 19, 2004:** The SPY closes substantially below the 200-day moving average. The 50-day moving average is ≥1 percent therefore the five-day rule is begun. Before the fifth day of the five-day rule the 50-day moving average drops to <1 percent of the 200-day moving average and on the fourth day of the five-day rule on July 23, 2004, we are forced to close all position with the SPY at 108.96.

The previous closing high was on June 23, 2004, at 114.75. The lowest low after we closed was on August 13, 2004, at 106.59. This was not a 10 percent correction from the previous closing high to the lowest low. Therefore we will use the 200-day moving average as our trigger to reenter the market.

**September 2, 2004:** The SPY closed substantially above the 200-day moving average and the five-day rule begins. On September 10, 2004, we reenter the market at 113.06.

**October 21, 2004:** On September 22, 2004, again the SPY closes below the 200-day moving average. But this time because the 50-day moving average is below the 200-day moving average, we are no longer using the 200-day moving average as our trigger line. The 50-day moving average is our trigger line. On September 23, 2004, the SPY closes below the 50-day moving average. But the five-day rule fails and we are still in the market. But on October 14, 2004, the SPY again closes substantially below the 50-day moving average and we begin the five-day rule. On October 21, 2004, the SPY is still below the 50-day moving average and again we close all positions at 111.24.

This is the only time in 15 years that we were whipsawed.

**November 3, 2004:** On October 27, 2004, the SPY closes above the 200-day moving average at 112.88. At the end of the five-day rule the SPY closes above the top of the candle body of the trigger day of October 27. We reenter the market on November 3, 2004, at 114.98. This normally would have been a one and done. But by the time the upper limit was reached the 50-day moving average was already above 1 percent of the 200-day moving average. Therefore trading was continued.

**October 13, 2005:** Between April 15, 2005, and May 13, 2005, there were several dips below the 200-day moving average, but each time the five-day rule kept us in the market. On October 6, 2005, there was a substantial close below the 200-day moving average and begins the five-day rule. On October 13, 2005, all positions are closed at 117.43.

**November 8, 2005:** On October 31, 2005, the SPY closes above the 200-day moving average at 120.13 and on November 7, 2005, it closes above the top of the candle body of the trigger day which was October 31. We reenter the market at 122.23.

**June 15, 2006:** On June 8, 2006, there is a substantial close below the 200-day moving average and five days later on June 15, 2006, we close all our positions at 126.12.

**August 2, 2006:** On June 29, 2006, the SPY closed substantially above the 200-day moving average. But five days later even though it is still above the 200-day moving average it did not close above the top of the candle body of the trigger day which was June 29. Nor did it close above the trigger day on a rolling five-day rule. As such we did not reenter the market.

On July 26, 2006, the SPY again closed substantially above the 200-day moving average and five days later on August 2, 2006, it was still above the top of the candle body of the trigger day of July 26. We reentered the market at 128.08. The upper limit is reached and no more trading until the 50-day moving average is ≥1 percent of the 200-day moving average. This is a one and done.

**September 20, 2006:** The 50-day moving average is ≥1 percent of the 200-day moving average. We again reenter the market at 132.51.

**November 15, 2007:** On November 8, 2007, the precursor to the biggest bear market since the Great Depression was taking place. The SPY closed at 147.16, below the 200-day moving average. But the 50-day moving average was still ≥1 percent of the 200-day moving average. Five trading days later on November 15, 2007, all positions were closed at 145.54. The previous highest close was on October 9, 2007, at 156.48 which was the record highest close for the SPY until that time. We were out at 145.54. That was within 10.94 points of the record highest close. At the time no one could foretell what was about to happen. The bear was about to strike. And the housing crisis was about to bring down an entire economy.

Briefly on December 6, 2007, the SPY closed substantially above the 200-day moving average but even though five days later it was above the 200-day moving average, the close was below the top of the candle body of the trigger day, December 6. As such we did not reenter the market.

**April 8, 2008:** On April 1, 2008, after more than a 10 percent correction the SPY substantially closes above the 50-day moving average. Five days later on April 8, 2008, the SPY is still above the top of the candle body of the trigger day of April 1. We reenter the market at 136.82. The upper limit is reached and it is a one and done.

**April 2, 2009:** The downward slide was a relentless bear, poking from time to time briefly above the 50-day moving average, never lasting through the five-day rule. On March 23, 2009, a year later the SPY closed substantially above the 50-day moving average and the five-day rule was begun. In order for the fifth day to be above the top of the candle body of the trigger day, it required a rolling five-day rule. On April 2, 2009, the SPY closed above the top of the candle body of the trigger day of March 26. We reentered the market at 83.43. This is a one and done.

**June 30, 2009:** On June 30, 2009, the 50-day moving average was ≥1 percent of the 200-day moving average and we reentered the market at 91.95.

**May 28, 2010:** On May 20, 2010, the SPY closed substantially below the 200-day moving average and we began the five-day rule count. On the fifth day it closed barely above the 200-day moving average so we waited one more day using a rolling five-day rule. The sixth day, May 28, 2010, was still below the 200-day moving average so all positions were closed.

A correction did technically take place as of May 24, 2010, but it actually doesn't matter since the 50-day moving average is above the 200-day moving average at the potential point of reentry. Therefore the 200-day moving average is the reentry trigger line. This would be the trigger line in this instance whether a correction had taken place or not.

On June 15, 2010, there was a substantial close above the 200-day moving average, but the five-day rule failed and we did not reenter the market.

Even though we did not reenter the market, there was a wave up above the 200-day moving average. Now that the 50-day moving average is moving below the 200-day moving average we must remeasure to see if there is a correction from the last wave up above the 200-day moving average.

That last wave up that was above the 200-day moving average closed on June 17, 2010, at 112.14. Therefore in order to have a correction the lowest low will have to be below 100.93. (112.14 × 0.90) On July 1, 2010, the SPY reached the lowest low at 101.13. Therefore a correction did not take place and we will use the 200-day moving average as the trigger line for our next possible reentry.

On August 2, 2010, there was a substantial close above the 200-day moving average at 112.76. We began the five-day rule count. On August 9, 2010, the fifth day, the SPY was above the top of the candle body of the trigger day of August 2. But it was only slightly above by a mere 0.23. In addition it formed a gap up and a doji. A doji looks like a cross with a small body crossing the high and low (✝).

A gap up indicates that there was initial support for a higher price. The price then continued to go up from the open then was beaten back by sellers and then went lower than the open. Buyers tried to support and there was a battle which ended with neither side winning, and it closed about where it opened which is what forms the cross. This means that there was not enough support in the face of selling to continue to push the SPY higher. A gap up followed by a doji then the next day a gap down is a very bearish sign. In the face of this it would pay to wait one more day and see if there is a gap down and use a rolling five-day rule to the sixth day.

As it turned out the sixth day was a gap down. The close was also lower than the top of the candle body of the trigger day. This was followed by a substantial downturn all the way down to a low of 104.29 on August 25, 2010.

Because of the last move above the 200-day moving average we must recalculate to see if there is a correction from that point even though we did not reenter the market.

That last wave up that was above the 200-day moving average closed on August 9, 2010, at 112.99. Therefore in order to have a correction the lowest low will have to be below 101.69. (112.99 × 0.90) On August 25, 2010, the SPY reached the lowest low at 104.95. Therefore a correction did not take place and we will use the 200-day moving average as the trigger line for our next possible reentry.

**September 20, 2010:** On September 13, 2010, the SPY closed substantially above the 200-day moving average and we began the five-day rule count. On September 20, 2010, it was above the highest point of the candle body of the trigger day at 114.21 so we reentered the market. This was a one and done.

Even though it was a one and done, we didn't have to wait long because the market went straight up. By the time the upper limit was reached, the 50-day moving average had previously gone above 1 percent of the 200-day moving average. This had occurred on October 20, 2010, at 117.87. Therefore when the upper limit was reached we simply continued to trade.

**August 3, 2011:** On August 2, 2011, the SPY closed at 132.57. The next day on August 3, 2011, there was a dramatic drop and the SPY gaped open at 125.66. If we multiply 132.57 × 0.95, we get 125.94. The SPY made a low of 123.53. This means that from the close of the previous day to the low of August 3, 2011, the SPY had dropped in excess of 5 percent in one trading session. It is time to pull the rip cord and get out. But don't panic initially. What normally happens on a day like this is that after the initial panic the market will recover somewhat. This of course is not guaranteed. Wait until 3:30 p.m. and see what happens. Regardless we are going to exit all positions before the close.

The market did rally off the lows and actually closed very close to the high for the day at 126.17. All positions were closed.

**October 18, 2011:** The previous *closing high* before the drop occurred on July 22, 2011, at 134.58. If we multiply 134.58 × 0.90, we get 121.12. Now we look for the *lowest low* after we closed our positions. This occurred on October 4, 2011, at 107.43, substantially below a 10 percent correction. This means that we will use the 50-day moving average as our trigger line for reentry.

On October 10, 2011, the SPY crossed above the 50-day moving average. But it was not substantial. We waited until the next day, October 11, 2011, and there was a substantial crossover. We began the five-day rule. On October 18, 2011, the SPY was above the top of the body of the candle of October 11, 2011, at 122.58. Therefore we reentered the market. This is a one and done assuming that the upper limit is reached. The expected move was about 4.95 which made the upper limit 127.53. This was reached on October 27, 2011, when the market made a high of 129.42 and closed at 128.63. We are now out of the market until such time as the 50-day moving average is ≥1 percent of the 200-day moving average.

**January 31, 2012:** The 50-day moving average became ≥1 percent of the 200-day moving average on January 31, 2012. We reentered the market at 131.32.

The market then continued to go up almost the entire year. On November 8, 2012, and November 9, 2012, there was a dip below the 200-day moving average, but it was not substantial. On November 9, 2012, it did dip initially what would be considered substantially, but it closed the day almost on the 200-day moving average line. Again, don't be a slave to the pennies. We waited one more day. On November 12, 2012, it moved back above the 200-day moving average. And on November 13, 2012, it did close substantially below the 200-day moving average. The five-day rule was begun.

The five-day rule failed to get us out on each of the rolling subsequent days and as such we did not exit the market. The SPY then continued to go up.

The market continued to go up for more than 3½ years. The SPY finally dipped below the 200-day moving average on August 20, 2015, and the 50-day moving average was <1 percent of the 200-day moving average. We closed all positions.

**November 1, 2013:** The detailed five-year analysis of The Non-Timing Trading System begins on November 1, 2013.

## How to Start

Now that you have all this information I'm sure you're anxious to get started. Before you make your first trade there are a few things that you need to be aware of. One of the worst things that can happen is for you to jump right in and make your first trade and then have the market go down and catch your lower limit. What would this do to you emotionally? Without any real experience to guide you, will you go ahead and make that first cover? What happens then if the market continues to go down and hit your next lower limit? Will your faith in the system be shaken at that point?

The first trade in a new system is vitally important. Being successful in that first trade will give you the confidence that will see you through downturns. Therefore you need to know where the market is and where it has been before you make that first trade.

In order to give that first trade an advantage it needs to be made after a lower limit has already been touched. The question is how do you determine this? This is not readily apparent because the upper and lower limits are created after a trade is made. But you haven't made a trade yet. Therefore we have to pretend that we have.

Where is the market at this point? Is it in an uptrend and making new highs? Is it moving sideways? Or is it going down? Let's look at each of these major types of markets and see how we can best enter.

Markets that are in an uptrend tend to go up then retrace then continue to make a new high and then retrace, and so on. Each peak in an up market is higher than the previous peak. See Figure 9.1.

Sometimes markets are moving sideways meaning there is no discernible trend. In this case each peak may be higher or lower than the previous peak. It will seem as though the market is moving through a channel. See Figure 9.2.

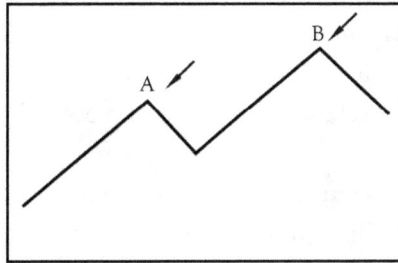

*Figure 9.1 Up market*

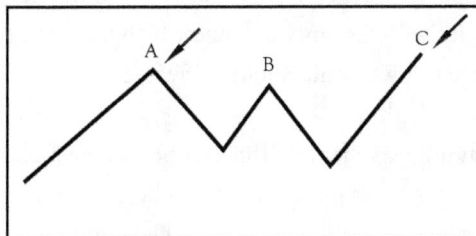

*Figure 9.2 Sideways market*

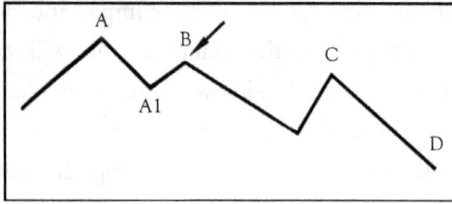

*Figure 9.3 Down market*

Of course markets move down. In a down market each peak is lower than the previous peak followed by a low which is lower than the previous low. See Figure 9.3.

Our challenge is to find a point from which we will create a pretend lower limit. Let's begin with a market that is moving up. Look at Figure 9.1. Every time a market makes a new high, use that new high as the point from which you establish a potential lower limit. If that lower limit is not reached then continue creating new lower limits from each new high. Notice point A in Figure 9.1 is from where a potential lower limit would be created. The market failed to reach that lower limit, therefore as the market was making new highs new lower limits would be created as indicated from point B. This will continue until a lower limit is reached.

The question arises as to how to find a 30-day expected move if we are already past that date in real time. You can use Think or Swim's "Thinkback" feature found in the Analyze tab. Just set your date to the date in question and you can see what the expected move was then for all of the option chains.

Now look at a sideways market using our example in Figure 9.2. From point A a new lower limit would be established. The market fails to reach the lower limit and then rallies to point B. But point B is not higher than point A. Therefore a new lower limit would not be established from point B. The lower limit established from point A is still in effect. The market still fails to reach the lower limit and a new high occurs at point C. Here from point C a new lower limit would be created. This will continue until a lower limit is reached.

Let's look at a down market. This can be the most challenging. The reason is because it creates the question of where do you begin. In an up market or in a sideways market you always begin with the last new high. Look at Figure 9.3. Assume that we are currently at point D. We look at the high at point A and from there we create a lower limit. But we see that the lower limit was reached at point A1. There is nothing we can do about that because we are now at point D, lower than we were at point A1. Since point A to A1 reached its lower limit, we are going to pretend that point A to A1 did not exist. Therefore we must go to our next peak which is point B. From here a new lower limit would be created and will be the lower limit that will be in effect until it is reached. We do not create a lower limit from point C because it is not higher than point B.

Once your pseudo-lower limit is reached, that is where you will enter the market for the first time. This will give you your best chance of being successful on your first trade. At least here you are buying in at a low (notice that I did not say *the low*) instead of at a high point. There obviously is no guarantee that the market will not go lower. But at least we are better off than if we had purchased at the high. The market may continue to go down and reach the lower limit that we established after we bought. But at least here it will be our first lower limit that we are covering, not our second. And remember that as the market is moving downward, volatility creates a safeguard in our mathematical model because it is increasing. This means that the distance to the next lower limit will be expanding. And if there is a third lower limit (in our case it will be the second), there is a good chance that it will temporarily force us out of the market anyway.

How close to the lower limit does it have to actually get? If we were actually in the market then the answer to this question is to the penny. When we are actually in the market not only does it actually have to reach the lower limit before we cover but it must still be there by 3:30 p.m. (one half hour before the market closes).

But in our case we are simply looking for a good place to enter the market for the first time. We are already becoming impatient and we want to get started. There is no actual magic about upper and lower limits. They are fluid because each day the upper and lower limits will change. The rules that establish the upper and lower limits were created because they give you a 60 percent chance or better that one of them will actually be touched within a two-month period.

With that in mind I will go ahead and enter the market once it is within a dollar of being reached. Let's assume that the lower limit is

207.16. Let's assume that the market is now at 207.92. I would go ahead and enter the market. Remember we're not really trying to find the absolute best time to enter the market, we're simply trying to increase our odds of being successful. At the presumed 207.92 we're getting very close to a lower limit. It would be a shame, being that close, to have to wait another three weeks before we could enter the market.

One final point needs to be made. Once a pseudo-lower limit has been created you need to go ahead and pretend that you are making the trade. This means that you must write down the expiration month that you are using for that pseudo-trade. This is important in an extremely long sideways market where the lower limit has not been reached for a couple of months. Remember that if you were actually in the market then you would have to close out all positions 30 days prior to expiration and establish a new upper and lower limit. You should do this with the pseudo-lower limit as well. Once your pseudo-entry point is 30 days from expiration then a new pseudo-lower limit should be established.

# CHAPTER 10

# Summary

The key to The Non-Timing Trading System is the process not the strategy itself or any strategy you might devise. The process is designed to keep you in the market when appropriate and to get you out and keep you out when the market is dangerous. It is also designed to recoup the inevitable losses that will occur while at the same time not continuously increasing your exposure during a major correction or a bear market.

The strategy that we have chosen has the advantage of adjusting the risk up or down with the resulting change in potential gain. If you want the strategy to have less risk and less reward then narrow the spread.

If you are just beginning and are unsure of the system or are new at buying and selling options, then it is recommended that you begin with a narrow spread. You can even make it as narrow as a one point spread. You are beginning trading as though you only had $500 available. You won't make a lot of money, but your mistakes will not cost you a lot and you are not putting a lot of money at risk.

Practice! Practice! Practice! This is the best advice you will receive. One way to practice is to use Think or Swim's "Thinkback." It is found under the Analysis tab. Begin with a different date than the tutorial trades used. When you begin with a different date it will have its own expected move which will create a different close or cover. Eventually as the market goes up it will even out and work out, but it will give you a completely different experience.

When you have done five years on your own creating the buying and selling of the required options, then you will have a good handle on not only the system, but also the procedures in Think or Swim.

Another way to practice is to use Think or Swim's "On Demand." This is an intraday database that will give you a real-time feel intraday as you buy and sell options. The only problem with "On Demand" is that if the option did not trade that day it will not execute in "On Demand" even if you are willing to pay more than the ask when you buy or willing to sell for less than the bid. This is a bug in an otherwise fantastic system for practicing. Hopefully it will be corrected so that you can force an execution at the appropriate ask or bid.

No matter how much you practice, if real money is not involved it is not the same feeling emotionally and psychologically. But you don't have to risk a lot of money to get the true feeling of trading. Don't risk so much that you cannot bring yourself to follow the system. If you do then that is when things will go very badly for you.

Don't try to out-think the market or try to predict it. It is just too complicated.

Follow the system.

# About the Author

**George O. Head** has a Master's degree in administration from Stetson University. He is first and foremost a teacher having taught computer science at the college level and high school levels as well as foreign language. For 20 years he consulted with and taught architects, engineers, and manufacturers complex computer software programs and consulted on financial management and systems integration. He has the ability to explain even the most complex concepts in easy-to-understand terms.

In the late 1970s Mr. Head was Business Manager with a school district near Austin, Texas. His responsibilities included not only the district's financial accounting, but also the investments of district funds during a time of hyperinflation.

In 1980, Mr. Head founded Associated Market Research and developed Integrated Management Systems which computerized and integrated financial accounting, time accounting, and job costing for architects and engineers. He has written six other books on financial management and computer-aided design which have been published in several languages. For 14 years he wrote monthly for a national computer magazine and was a guest contributor to another. In 2000 he returned to teaching and retired in 2010.

## Disclaimer and Risk Disclosure

This book is not intended to provide investment or financial advice or make investment recommendations. Nothing contained in this book is to be construed as a recommendation for any particular security, transaction, or investment.

Securities used as examples in this book are for illustrative purposes only. It is not recommended that you buy or sell any security. Past performance may not be indicative of future performance. All information provided in this book is for educational purposes only and does not imply, express, or guarantee future returns.

Trading securities can involve high risk and the loss of any funds invested. Investment information provided may not be appropriate for all investors and is provided without respect to individual investor financial sophistication, financial situation, investing time horizon, or risk tolerance.

Options trading is generally more complex than stock trading and may not be suitable for some investors. Some option strategies can result in the loss of more than the original amount invested. Before trading options, a person should review the document, Characteristics and Risks of Standardized Options, available from your broker or any exchange on which options are traded.

The example trades in this book are simulated. Simulated performance results have certain inherent limitations. Unlike an actual performance record, simulated results do not represent actual trading. Also, since the trades in this book have not actually been executed, the results stated may have under- or overcompensated for the impact, if any, of certain market factors such as lack of liquidity. Simulated trading programs in general are also subject to the fact that they are designed with the benefit of hindsight. No representation is being made that any account will or is likely to achieve profits or losses similar to those shown.

The author and The Non-Timing Trading System assume no responsibility for actions taken by the reader. We are not providing investment advice. We do not make any claims, promises, or guarantees that any suggestion will result in a profit, loss, or any other desired result. The reader assumes all risk, including but not limited to the risk of trading losses.

# Index